SCIENTIFIC MALPRACTICE

THE CREATION/EVOLUTION DEBATE

IVAN L. ZABILKA

SCIENTIFIC MALPRACTICE:
The Creation/Evolution Debate
Copyright © 1992 by Ivan L. Zabilka
Published by Bristol Books

First Edition, July 1992

Unless otherwise indicated, all Scripture quotations are from the *Holy Bible, New International Version* © 1973, 1978 by the International Bible Society. Used by permission.

Cover design by David E. Caldwell.

ISBN 0-917851-17-X

Printed in the United States of America.

BRISTOL BOOKS
An imprint of Bristol House, Ltd.
2201 Regency Road, Suite 301 ◆ Lexington, KY 40503
phone: (606) 276-4583
fax: (606) 276-5365
To order, call our toll-free line: 1-800-451-READ

TABLE OF CONTENTS

ACKNOWLEDGEMENTS

The statements of participants in a great debate require careful analysis and evaluation. The creation/evolution debate exhibits an excess of bias on both sides, and the historian has a daunting task in maintaining balance in presenting the evidence. I have sought to be fair and yet make clear my own support of evangelical Christianity in conjunction with acceptance of the methods of the scientific community. Several friends have read all or parts of the manuscript. They do not all agree with my conclusions, or share my perspective, and consequently I have been unable to accept all their advice. I am profoundly thankful, however, for that advice and assistance, and accept the remaining errors of fact and interpretation as my own.

I wish to thank Edward H. Madden, Ph.D., former Professor of Philosophy at the State University of New York at Buffalo for reading chapters two, three, seven and eight and saving me from several embarrassing flaws. I am indebted to Carl Esbeck, J.D., Associate Professor of Law at the University of Missouri-Columbia for reading chapters one, two, three and six and improving the clarity of those chapters. My mentor Eric C. Christianson, Ph.D., Associate Professor of History at the University of Kentucky, read chapters one, two, three and eight and suggested many clarifications of definition and improvements in the arguments. My friend for over 32 years, J. Paul Ray, Ph.D., former Professor of Chemistry and Earth Science at Asbury College, Wilmore, Kentucky, read the entire work and made many helpful suggestions. Gilbert Crouse, Ph.D., Professor of Economics at Anderson College, Anderson Indiana, and Loal Ames, Vice-President for Non-Traditional Programs at Roberts Wesleyan College in Syracuse, New York, read most of the manuscript and made many useful comments. Elizabeth Gardner, Director of the English Communications Laboratory at Asbury College saved me from many egregious errors of various types. My adult children, Eric and Laura, and my daughter-in-law Kelly have been patient with me throughout the production of this work. They have encouraged and prodded and in general done whatever was needed to keep me going. I also thank James Robb, Editor-in-Chief of Bristol House, Ltd. and David Cupps, Editorial Assistant for untold hours of effort in making this a better book than it would have been without their help.

This book is respectfully and lovingly dedicated to the memory of Cecil B. Hamann, Ph.D., who was for over three decades Professor of Biology at Asbury College, and who first awakened in me the necessity of wrestling with the major issues and thinking clearly about them.

I request something of my readers as well. This is neither an easy nor a comfortable book. Some of the issues are complicated and chapter four will be a mystery to some of my readers. I ask that you make the effort anyway. I consider myself a gentle person. My mode of life is to flee controversy, yet I have chosen to write a controversial book because I believe strongly in what I say. I mean no harm to those I oppose, and I believe they sincerely seek to do right, yet I believe they cause damage to the church of Jesus Christ and have so stated. If you are seeking light reading save your time and read no further. If you wish to wrestle with one of the many challenges facing the church I have done my best to provide you with the starting place.

Ivan L. Zabilka, Ph.D.
Lexington, Kentucky

Dimensions of the Debate

Most Christians consider themselves "creationists." They do so because one of the basic doctrines of the Christian faith is that God is the originator of the universe. Many Christians have only the vaguest notion of how God might have done this creative act; could evolution have been part of the process? Many Christians are unaware that during the last three decades the meaning of "creationist" has changed, and they are shocked to find scientists hostile if they suggest they hold creationist beliefs. Some scientists are also surprised to find that not all Christians adhere to the position of the group of Christians who have co-opted the word "creationist" for themselves. In the pages that follow, we will explore what is happening between the sciences and faith as a result of the new Creationists and suggest some ways out of the tensions that have resulted.

During the 1970s a movement called "scientific creationism" gained wide attention, both within and beyond the Christian community. The most familiar proponents of this belief system present many claims in opposition to the positions of the scientific community. Among the most troublesome assertions by Creationists are that the movement represents *the* valid Christian position; that Christianity is only partially or inadequately understood if the Creationist position is not adopted; and that the creation/evolution conflict is *the* strategic issue confronting the Church today.[1] They are essentially claiming that if a person does not believe that the universe was created 10,000 years ago, one has only an inadequate faith or has been duped by the scientific community. According to surveys, the Creationists have succeeded in convincing a majority of Americans that their position is so important that it ought to be presented in the public schools. Presumably an even greater majority of Christians are sympathetic to the Creationist effort.

The perspective presented here is that Creationism is undeserving of the prominent position it has gained. After considering the evidence, Evangelical Christians will find that Creationism is not a satisfactory alternative to the atheism implicit in some expositions of origins by evolutionary scientists. Creationism is an inadequate alternative because it rejects much of modern science without sufficient justification or adequate alternatives. Furthermore, the Creationist position is the result of an inappropriate method of interpreting the Bible. For several centuries Protestants from a variety of perspectives have sought a synthesis of science and faith that preserves the unity and integrity of both the "natural revelation" (the physical world to which the methods of science have been applied) and the "special revelation" (which tells of the spiritual condition of Man and the means of salvation as presented in the Bible). The quest for this synthesis continues to be the viable position for Christians in the effort to understand the problems surrounding the study of origins.[2]

Suggesting that fellow Christians are in error requires strong evidence. Most of this book summarizes the evidence that the Creationists are wrong. More briefly, certain points are addressed where evolutionists have extended their conclusions beyond the evidence and have engaged in speculative thinking. The intent of the author is to focus upon the traditionally orthodox Christian position that science and religion are compatible and to provide a more adequate interpretation of the relevant biblical passages that allows us to keep the progress that modern science has made in understanding origins.

Arguments of the Creationists

The evidence of the inadequate arguments of the Creationists has accumulated rapidly in recent years. The surprising and most obvious differences between scientists and Creationists is the rejection by the latter of major portions of standard science. This rejection extends to the evidence of the antiquity of the Earth and the universe in favor of a span of approximately 10,000 years. Standard geology is discounted by Creationists, who argue that the dating of fossil finds by means of the radioactive elements that they contain is unreliable. Creationists reject the standard interpretation of the geological column (the arrangement of the rock layers of the Earth's crust in chronological order with the oldest on the bottom) as evidence of the pattern of evolution and evidence for the antiquity of the Earth. With so little time since the Creation, the Creationists reject the succession of ice ages, shifts in the Earth's magnetic field and continental drift. Since the Creationists reject the biological evidence of the evolution of species, one of their most shocking conclusions is that all life forms are contemporaneous; that is, while some have perished, they all co-existed at some time in the past 10,000 years—clearly in opposition to the fossil record.

The Creationist rejection of standard science is not, however, confined to the controversial issue of antiquity, but in recent years has extended into other branches of science as well, including astronomy. The Creationists have increasingly been forced to reject astronomical evidence supporting the great age of the universe, with some indicating that the universe was created with only the appearance of great age. A sense of dismay is the frequent Christian response when it becomes clear that the Creationists are actually proposing that God created a natural world which contains evidence that deceives its observers. Some Creationists ignore the standard interpretations and controls of physics by misapplying the closed-system second law of thermodynamics to an open system. A "closed system" means that no energy enters from outside, and no energy escapes the system. In informal terms the "second law" states that the energy available in the system is gradually converted from usable to unusable forms until it is exhausted. An extension of this principle is that complexity will normally decrease as the available energy declines. The Earth, however, is not a closed system since the Sun continuously infuses additional energy into the Earth's system—a fact that Creationists conveniently ignore. These themes will be more fully developed in chapter four as we attempt to understand what they believe and why the scientific community is so adamant in rejecting their position. The intention of the author is not an exhaustive treatment of the scientific issues which are difficult for the non-scientist to master, but this work is a survey of these differences so they can be clearly understood. The magnitude of what is at stake for the sciences and the faith should be clear.

The confrontation with science is compounded by the Creationists' acceptance of tenets incompatible with the evidence of current science. The unusual interpretations of the Creationists are primarily concentrated in geology and geophysics. Some of the more important incompatibilities with science include the unverifiable assumption, mentioned above, of variable decay rates of radioactive substances. Physicists have found no evidence that the rate at which a radioactive substance decays into stable isotopes is not constant with time. Creationists have asserted the probability of variable decay rates without having a theory indicating why they should vary.

A second Creationist position incompatible with science is that all fossilized forms have their origin in the biblical Flood. While most theories of fossil formation take into account the role of catastrophes in the conditions necessary to create fossils, the evidence for the age of the universe and the distribution of fossils eliminates the possibility of all fossils being formed in one event 8,000 or so years ago. The Creationists have not presented adequate evidence or a supporting theory to indicate the process of rapid general fossil formation, although they do appeal to short-term intense heat and pressure to create coal. One implication of their position is that all life forms existed at the same time in the past. Consequently they have searched for evidence of the contemporaneous existence of life forms where science says there should be none. The necessity of protecting the 10,000 year chronology forces the Creationists to such anti-scientific positions.

Biblical Issues

Were the non-scientific character of Creationism its only difficulty, Christians could cheerfully leave the critique of Creationism in the hands of the scientific community, which has in recent years written many books against the Creationists. However, there is a second concern for Evangelical Christians who wish to take seriously the Bible's message about Man's condition and the means of salvation. This concern is that Creationism is a departure from the centuries-old core of traditional Christian beliefs held by that vast portion of Christianity that falls under the labels of orthodox, conservative and evangelical.

The primary reason for their rejection of science and acceptance of unsubstantiated theories stems from their interpretation of the Bible. The Creationists, in their enthusiasm for the truth of the Bible, are drawn into an untenable conclusion. Since the Bible in Genesis One speaks of origins, it must speak the truth about origins. Since science speaks of origins differently, and the Bible is true, then science must be false. In essence, this argument makes the Bible a scientific text, even though it was written three and a half millenia before the advent of science. The unbelievable result is that the Bible is expected to conform to the standards of science. The argument, of course, ignores that the Bible is written in non-technical terms explaining why we do not worship the created world or things in it, rather than providing a technical explanation of the method of creation.

An initial problem with Creationism is that it is founded on an inappropriate hermeneutic. Hermeneutics is the methodology of interpreting documents, applied to many historical documents but most extensively to the Bible in order to determine the meaning to the original audience and the relevance to the present audience. In both its approach to the Bible and to scientific sources, the Creationist movement depends upon a hermeneutic that is most commonly called "proof-texting." The essence of proof-texting is that the Creationist begins with a fixed conclusion, followed by a search to find quotations that will support the conclusion. This method produces neither good science nor good theology.

A second element in the inadequate interpretative method of the Creationists involves inadequate attention to the biblical context. At times it seems that any text that has the right words in it is a scientific text, regardless of the intention of the original author, the issue under consideration, or the type of literature in which the statement is embedded. Creationists routinely ignore the primacy of the meaning for the original audience in the process of interpreting a biblical passage. This is especially true with regard to

Genesis One, which was directed toward the problem of polytheism, not the issue of origins. The consequence of this neglect is a disappointing emphasis upon the scientific meaning of a passage and an interpretation that is immune to the meaning of a passage to other times and other cultures. These issues will be more fully explored in chapter five and in the concluding chapter.

Creationist Political Objectives

Creationists must interpret not only the Bible, but history as well. The Enlightenment and religious toleration, two historical movements that have traditionally been held as positive movements in world history (including by Christians), must be reinterpreted as part of an evil conspiracy against Christians and the Bible. The Enlightenment, rather than breaking the inappropriate intellectual suppression practiced by some within the Roman Catholic Church, must be viewed as the evil parent of science, which is viewed as an enemy. Similarly, the growth of toleration, rather than being viewed as the movement which gave the Creationists themselves the right to challenge the scientific establishment, is viewed as an evil acceptance of cultural falsehoods.

Presumably the matter of greatest concern to most Christians is the Creationist distortion of the core of the Christian faith. Creationism enlists devotion to a cause that does not keep Christ's atonement for human sin as the central focus of the movement. Creationists have subordinated the divinity of Christ and his provision of deliverance from sin to one's position with regard to the method of creation as the dividing line for inclusion among believers.

The Creationists also displace the defense of the Christian faith, usually called polemics, moving the focus from the historical issues of the life of Christ and the origin of the Church to the issue of origin of the universe. The consequence is a change from issues in which the great debate is over clearly-defined ideological positions concerning the interpretation of the historical facts to an emphasis on more speculative issues in which the ideological differences are disguised or subordinated to the debate of elusive facts. In essence, the Creationists make the defense of the faith more difficult because they have moved the debate from the divinity of Christ to a more peripheral issue where their position is more vulnerable.

This vulnerability poses an important threat to the Church and its mission in the world. As the scientific community succeeds in exposing the invalidity of the Creationist movement, the disrepute falling upon them devolves upon the whole Church because of their persistent claim to be the true representatives of Christian faith. Further, their inadequate interpretive methodology with regard to the Bible leads a theologically unsophisticated society to assume that all Christian doctrine has been disproven by the efforts of the scientists in the area of origins.

The displacement of appropriate Christian emphases exposes the political objectives of the Creationist movement. The Creationists seek to use the power and reputation of the Church to force the state to legislate the movement's objectives. Attempting to use the state to accomplish its objectives appears likely to bring about state involvement in the affairs of the Creationist movement, which has happened with the State of California's intervention in the right of the Institute for Creation Research to grant degrees. Creationist resources have been used to initiate legal actions in an effort to get the courts to achieve what the Creationists could not do in competition with science. The consequence appears to be that Church and state have been involved in unnecessary legal action which could impair other legal efforts of the Church to defend itself against state intervention in educational matters of conscience.

Finally, the Creationist movement seeks to impose its views on society as a whole through the use of the doctrine of fairness, adopted from the broadcast industry. This doctrine indicates that opposing viewpoints must be granted equal time on the airwaves. Creationists have appealed to the sense of fairness of the American people to get their alternative before the public and in the schools. As will be demonstrated, they have been largely unsuccessful on the national level, but locally they have been very effective.

Inadequate science, an inappropriate hermeneutic and a political mentality free from the moderating influence of the Church have created a movement that does little honor to the Church and the God it seeks to serve. As a consequence, Creationism is not a satisfactory position for other Christians to adopt with regard to science. These issues are considered in detail in chapters six and seven.

Scientific Opposition to Creationism

All is not well, however, within the scientific community. When faced with Creationist opposition many scientists have organized to defend science and to eliminate any involvement of theological conceptions with it. The culmination of a century of attempts to separate science from religion has led to claims that science is all there is—a complete explanatory system for the world we see about us. This leaves the thoughtful Christian deeply dissatisfied.

The Creationists have sought to broaden the separation into a dichotomy consisting of these two choices: Creationism or atheistic evolution. The purpose is to lead the undecided into their perspective. Some scientists have willingly accepted the dichotomy, believing that the defeat of Creationism would undermine all Christian faith if the Creationists are allowed to represent themselves as the only viable alternative. Contrary to both sides in this debate, a third position that incorporates both science and faith explains more and integrates life better than either of the current polar alternatives.

Most contemporary scientists are relatively indifferent to religion in the performance of their duties. It intrudes little on the day-to-day activities of research, writing and teaching. But while most are indifferent, at least until threatened by a movement like Creationism, there are some scientists who show strong resentment toward religion (Christianity in particular) because of its claims to exclusive possession of the way of salvation. For some of these scientists, the rejection of the faith seems less a result of their scientific research than their choice of science as a career because it was free from influence by the faith. For some the resentment toward religion appears grounded in an emotional reaction to the simplistic undeveloped faith of their childhood. For others it appears rooted in the outmoded and distorted "warfare" concept of the relationship between religion and science. The Creationists' confrontational methodology in public debate has aggravated this perception.

Whatever the motivation, there is strong opposition on the part of some scientists to Christianity. With only "professionalism" to provide moral constraints, some of the stronger opponents of Christianity within the scientific community have twisted Christian positions, distorted the meaning and even the history of Christianity and attemped to obscure the weakness or nature of their own metaphysical underpinnings.

The theory of origins is one of the most speculative areas of modern science. Evidence is difficult to obtain because the geologic record has been modified extensively over time. Because the factual evidence is problematic, the presuppositions of the researcher play a more significant role than in other areas of science. Greater candor on the part of the scientific community would be helpful at this point. Some ardent evolutionists believe that the evidence pressed them to an anti-Christian position, when they in fact had an initial bias against God. Evolution is a means of combating Christianity and its claim upon their thoughts and devotion.

A Christian Alternative to Creationism

Fortunately, there is a Christian alternative to Creationism and atheistic evolution that is more metaphysically and logically tenable than either of these extremes. While Christian theology has long organized certain evidences for the existence of God, these are obviously rejected by the atheist. Interestingly, they are seldom met philosophically or logically, but are normally lampooned or dismissed as "old," as if that makes them unreliable or already refuted. What is difficult for some to admit is that the Christian metaphysic is as logically consistent as an atheistic one and is not arrived at by means of the consideration of the evidence. The decision about God's existence is the starting point, not the conclusion. It is an *a priori* assumption. For the Christian it is simply less difficult to comprehend how God could successfully interact with an orderly universe than it is to explain how the universe could be so orderly without an organizing intelligence behind it. Indeed, this is the "old" argument from design, which is as powerful now as when it was first proposed.

Christian alternatives to Creationism must take the Bible, the record of some of God's interaction with Man, very seriously. The text of the Bible has been more reliably protected and transmitted than any other ancient document. The evidence of the consistency and integration of these documents (collected over hundreds of years) and the unity of the message is overwhelming. To most Christians the message of the Bible concerning creation is clear. From the semi-poetic first chapter of Genesis through the historical narratives to the apocalyptic concluding chapters, the message is that God is active in the universe. Genesis One is probably the passage from the Bible that has received more attention than any other in recent years. There is no way to avoid serious considera-tion of it because it in presumed to say more about origins in one compact location than any other part of the Bible. We will consider this passage in the concluding chapter.

In addition to considering the importance of the Bible and its interpretation in establishing a viable Christian position concern-ing origins, we must also consider the role of science. Science is simply not all there is. Thought is more than synapses; life is more than chemical reactions; and the human is more than mere animal, possessing something more than just a greater amount of the characteristics of the animals. Man can reason, learn and remem-ber, all of which allow him to make decisions. As a consequence we are aware that science cannot answer many of the questions that arise in life; for example, scientists feel confident that the Big Bang took place some twenty billion years ago, but why it occurred at that moment is forever hidden. Science is much more adept at answering the "what" questions than the "why" questions. The spiritual nature of Man cannot be understood, nor can it be aided by science.

What then ought to be the Evangelical Christian attitude to-ward science, since some of the proponents of science oppose the metaphysical? Evangelicals will have little corrective influence on and less interaction with the scientific community if we continue to regard science as a threat or an enemy. As often stated by earlier Christian scholars, whatever in science relates to the physical universe will be compatible with the revelation of God in the created cosmos, if both are properly understood. We may expect God to be consistent, not capricious. It is only our limited understanding that sometimes makes his created universe appear so chaotic. The Christian effort should not be to invalidate the research of thousands of scholarly investigators in one sweep, but rather to identify properly and to draw attention to the inappropriate metaphysical assumptions of those who seek to destroy the faith.

The goal of this book is the presentation of an appropriate world view that seeks to integrate the natural and special revelation. Rejecting the extremes does not merely lead to a compromise in the middle but to a positive alternative to Creationism that makes sense and is true to both science and faith. The problems raised by the Creationists for the Church and the scientific community are significant.

Since this author is a historian and neither scientist nor theologian, this book will not answer all the scientific or theological questions. The goal is to expose some of the unfortunate results of the current debate and to look in the right direction for the answers. If I point some to a more sensible study of the issues I will have achieved my purpose. If I challenge some to think of significant issues that are new to them I will be delighted. In chapters two and three we will begin the process by looking at some historical information that helps us understand how we got where we are in this modern scientific and theological issue.

2

Identifying Creationism

Attitudes Toward Creationists

A few dozen leaders with perhaps as many as 18,000,000 followers, calling themselves Scientific Creationists, have convinced a majority of Americans that their view of origins ought to be taught alongside standard science in the public schools. In October of 1981 the Associated Press and NBC conducted a poll and found that 76% favored the presentation of both creation and evolution in the public classrooms.[1] This poll concluded that the Creationist appeal to the sense of fairness in the general public had convinced the public to cover all the alternatives in the schools in the hope that one was right. In 1982 Gallup conducted a national survey of beliefs concerning Creationism. The sample consisted of 1518 adults over the age of eighteen. Of those sampled 44% believed in the "biblical" account of creation within the last 10,000 years. This survey verified the difference between Catholics and Protestants. Among the Protestants surveyed, 49% accepted a recent creation, while 43% did not. Among the Catholics, 38% accepted the "biblical" account while 55% accepted evolution.[2]

More recent surveys have considered student opinion on college and university campuses. A 1985 survey at Ohio State University revealed that 62% of the student body accepted evolution, but a sizeable minority (25%) believed that scientists doubted evolution, even though publicly supporting it, and 22% believed that teaching naturalistic science led to the decay of American society. Once again, 80% supported equal time for Creationism in the public schools. Fifty-eight percent denied that adding discussion of Creationism would be introducing religion into the public schools.

At Oberlin College, highly academic and liberal in religion and politics, 89% of the students believed in evolution, and 92% believed that scientists believed evolution. But even at Oberlin, 56% thought Creationism should be taught in the schools. Toward the more conservative end of the political spectrum, at the University of Texas-Arlington, 28% of the student body held Creationist views, and 42% believed that evidence exists refuting evolution. While an exact percentage is not stated, the students at Texas overwhelmingly supported equal time for the Creationists. Clearly, Creationists have established equal time for Creationism as a majority view.[3]

Understanding who they are and what they believe will be a surprise to most Americans and to many Christians, who have given tacit approval to the concept that fairness entitles Creationists to equal time in the public school curriculum whenever the issue of origins is considered. The initial requirement is to understand just who the Creationists are.

Background of Creationists

Many Creationists differ from those supporting evolution in that they are not scientifically trained, but technologically trained. Most people are unaware that there is a difference between a scientist and a technologist, but not only is there a substantive difference, historically there has been strong rivalry. The first evidences are traceable to the scientific revolution of the mid-seventeenth century, but the intensity of the rivalry changed dramatically during the last half of the nineteenth century. After 1850 two developments became increasingly prominent in the history of science: the tendency toward professionalization, and the trend toward specialization. The first of these simply meant that it became possible to make a living working at science, usually on the college campus;

it later increased with government work through geological surveys and the Smithsonian Institution. The rapid expansion of the college system in the United States created many laboratories and numerous positions, enough to make full-time efforts in science possible. This meant that the long tradition of amateur involvement in "natural philosophy" (physical science) drew to a close. The professionalization process led to a sudden increase in the complexity of scientific theory, which in turn raised a barrier excluding the amateur.

Concurrently, in the mid-nineteenth century, there was also an explosion in technological advance. Based initially upon the steam engine and then upon precision machine manufacturing, mechanical invention dramatically intensified. The technological explosion was much more empirical than the scientific and was consequently much more open to the amateur. The public seldom distinguished between the scientific and the technological developments, which frequently overlapped with the same persons participating in both activities. During the twentieth century, however, the distinctions between science and technology have become more clear.

There are both philosophical and educational differences between the two groups.[4] Philosophically the scientist is trained to think abstractly and theoretically, in an exploratory and tentative fashion. The education in support of scientific methodology has both strong theoretical and research components. Stated simply, a scientific education tends to be developmental and historical in orientation.

The technologically trained person (including the engineer) confronts a different philosophical approach and a different educational system. Philosophically the dominant perspective is practicality. The alliance of technology with the business community leads to a focus on "what works," including matters of economy and efficiency. In educational matters the "how to" question is much more important than the "why does it work" type of question. While the scientist sees a spectrum of possibilities, the technically educated person is looking for the one best solution to a problem.

The distinction between scientists and technologists is revealing in the question of origins. Creationists are predominantly technologically educated, that is, they are engineers, medical personnel and computer technologists. By 1960, when the Creationist movement first attained prominence, a sizable minority of technicians and medical personnel were Christians, some of them Creationists. Only a handful of biologists, and only a few from the other sciences were Creationists, but among engineers, computer experts, and clinical (as opposed to research) physicians, many opposed evolution. With this base of respectability the Creationists launched a "scientific" case against evolution.

Tension between scientists and technologists arises when the indefiniteness, abstractness and reserved judgment of the scientist meet the practicality, results-orientation and singlemindedness of the technologist. The Creationist movement reflects this larger tension in that its debate with evolutionary science contains elements of the distrust and resentment of the technical community toward the "impracticality" of the scientists. Many of the Creationists engaged in "research", are actually pursuing projects for the business community far removed from the biological issues involved in the conflict. Many Creationist leaders reflect the practical orientation of their education in their own methods. They appear to resent the indefiniteness of science, especially when scientists debate each other about the different possibilities for the process of evolution. The Creationists mistake the debate over the process for doubt about evolution itself. They also appear to resent the relativism of science, which seldom comes to a set conclusion.

Creationists and Fundamentalism

The Creationists are Fundamentalist, with a strong commitment to traditional theology and especially to the error-free nature of the Bible. Fundamentalists have much in common with Evangelicals, but they tend to hold a rigidly and narrowly-defined stance with regard to the relation of the Church and society. Politically, the Fundamentalists are frequently associated with the "New Religious Right," although the two groups are not synonymous.[5]

The Creationist leaders and organizations draw their funding from Fundamentalist members of the Protestant churches. While nearly every denomination contains Creationists, the Baptists predominate. A uniting theme is a literal interpretation of certain passages in the Bible, emphasizing the "obvious" meaning with little regard for cultural or theological context. Literalism, combined with a technological orientation, leads to what is most frequently called a "proof-texting" approach to problem solving. For Creationists the Bible provides the one correct picture of reality, and the function of science is to provide the supporting evidence. There are few areas where Christians may legitimately differ, they say; differences mean that one is wrong. There are several consequences of this orientation, including a distorted sense of the importance of the present; if opinions in the past differed, they must be wrong. With simplicity as a standard in interpreting the Bible, they frequently descend into dogmatism.

Creationist Organizations

The organizations of the Creationists are parachurch, meaning they are outside the denominational structure of Protestant churches. They are independent of the control and moderating influences that might come from the leadership of the differently educated clergy. Since denominational ministers are not scientists or technologists, they are not encouraged to participate in Creationist gatherings. Thus, their political and legal agenda has received little input from church bodies, although their influence upon the Protestant church has been significant. While their books frequently indicate a concern for evangelism and the well-being of society, they give little consideration to the consequences of their program upon the Church. There are many different organizations, some with purely scientific purposes, some with educational objectives, others with lobbying and judicial goals.

The separatist nature of Creationism is apparent from the appearance of their work only in Creationist journals and in books from Creationist publishers. The Creationists have frequently claimed exclusion from normal scientific journals, but a survey revealed that of 135,000 articles submitted to scientific journals only 18 were Creationist and those 18 were predominantly by non-scientists. The results of Creationist research, if it is being done, is not being submitted to scientific journals.[6] They publish their positions without the usual peer review controls of the scientific community. Publication takes place without criticism from opposing viewpoints, the existence of which they would regard as a sign of weakness in the movement. There is little scientific assessment of the value of the work prior to publication.

While the current movement has approximately a seventy year history, dating to the publication of *The Fundamentals*, the present scientific Creationists are either unaware of their predecessors or choose not to acknowledge them. Evidence of their lack of awareness is that they frequently repeat arguments against evolution that have previously been scientifically refuted. They also appear to fail to attribute their arguments to the originators, especially if those originators were ministers rather than scientists.

Creationists appear to be scientifically, socially and religiously narrow, people who work diligently to preserve their views through private schools. More than 1000 schools belong to the American Association of Christian Schools and must affirm that they do not believe in evolution.[7] There is little effort toward balanced treatment in many of these schools, for evolution is seldom mentioned in any context other than that it is evil.

The Creationist leadership is a relatively small group of men clustered around a small group of organizations, but with an immense following. Among the more widely recognized names are Henry M. Morris, Director of the Institute for Creation Research (ICR); Duane Gish, Associate Director of the ICR; Garry Parker and Richard P. Bliss, both of the ICR; Kelly L. Segraves, Creation Science Research Center; Paul Ellwanger, Committee for Fairness in Education; and Harold S. Slusher, John W. Moore, Martin E. Clark, W.L. Wysong, and Robert E. Kofahl. These are the best known because of their writings or their public appearances. Morris and Gish are the most prolific authors among this group. These and the many other Creationists have produced in excess of 350 books outlining the Creationist position.[8]

Originally, the most prominent and best-financed organization was the Creation Research Society (CRS, based in Ann Arbor with 2,500 members), which broke away from the American Scientific Affiliation (ASA) in 1963 because the ASA was too sympathetic to evolution. The ASA, still in existence, is an organization of practicing scientists who are Christians. Other Creationist organizations include the Creation Science Research Center (CSRC, San

Diego) which split away from the CRS, the Institute for Creation Research (ICR, San Diego), which has currently emerged as the most powerful organization, the Bible-Science Association (Minneapolis), the Creation Social Studies and Humanities Society and the Citizens for Fairness in Education, a political action group. There are others, but these are the best organized, the most prolific publishers, and the most politically active.

What Creationists Believe

While detailed specifics of Creationist belief will be considered in the following chapters, a brief overview is helpful. In sympathy with Francis Schaeffer, a major conservative intellectual, they attribute the ills of the Church and society to social and intellectual changes that resulted from the Enlightenment.

The most sweeping Creationist concern is devoted to the general concept of evolution and its application to all aspects of human activity, which they regard as a consequence of the Enlightenment. They frequently confuse biological evolution with Social Darwinism, which is the application of evolutionary development and the concept of "survival of the fittest" to social structure. Evolution is presumed to be the intellectual fountainhead of many other evils including relativism, mechanistic and positivistic philosophies in the sciences, and determinism in philosophy. To Creationists this litany of dependent evils is sufficient to explain the danger of the theory.

The particular trend that has led to the currently degenerate state of society, they say, is the overemphasis upon science (or naturalism) and the neglect of the Bible. Unlike traditional Christianity, which regards the natural world and the special revelation as two valid means of revelation, the Creationist finds the Bible, literally interpreted, more important. The consequence of this belief is that Creationism is assumed to be the most obvious and effective means of restoring a godly society.[9]

Since the polls reveal that a majority accept the right of Creationists to equal time in the science classroom, it is appropriate to summarize Creationist beliefs. The following five major points are based on Creationist organizations' membership statements and common language in many recent legislative proposals.

1) The Earth is only about ten thousand years old. Modern geology and radiometry are in error when they claim evidence to the contrary, and astronomical measurements have no true bearing on the age of the universe or the Earth.

2) The "kinds" mentioned in Genesis 1:24-25 are fixed. These "kinds" are not equivalent to species, and most Creationists allow for variations within these broad groupings ("microevolution") while rejecting movement from one "kind" to another ("macroevolution"). In connection with this point, Creationists stress that Man and the apes are of different "kinds" and therefore are not related.

3) Fossils are the result of the universal flood several thousand years ago. Fossil distribution is due to varying deposition at that time rather than being a result of evolutionary development.

4) The obvious complexity of life is by simple probability impossible; the inherent design necessitates a Designer. That Designer created all of the Earth's complex life forms at one time, and many of them have survived to this day.

5) The universe and everything in it was created from nothing. God, not matter, is eternal.

The argument from design and creation from nothing have been traditional elements of Christian theology. The other parts of the Creationist position are modern developments in a technological society that would have had little meaning to Christians prior to the middle of the last century.

The Historical Development of Creationism

Creationism is primarily an American phenomenon. More than any other country, the United States has taken faith seriously without at the same time establishing any one faith as the state religion. Religious toleration as an ideal has enjoyed more practical application in the U.S. than has been the case elsewhere, although intolerance has been present in great measure as well.[10] Because of the intensity of religious sentiment in the United States, the Christian faith, in varying degrees, has permeated the social fabric. There is, as a consequence, some internal tension in American society between personal commitment to faith and the ideal of toleration. Creationism capitalizes upon this tension in American social and political thought.

Creationism, approximately in its present form, has existed nearly seventy years, since it became clearly defined when the schism between modernist and fundamentalist thought grew strong in the late nineteenth century.[11] Beginning in the early 1800s two separate trends emerged. The German scholarly community began to apply critical and analytical methods to the Bible. Linguistics, philology, source and literary type analysis, and comparative literary methods were all part of the process. In the hands of certain members of this academic community who were opposed to the abuses within the Church in their day, some criticism took a negative turn, including extreme antagonism to traditional Christian faith. By the 1890s a polarization formed within Christian thought between those for whom the Bible was still the Word of God, delivered in times past to selected individuals, and those for whom the Bible was just another human book around which an amazing mythology had grown. The former group was progressively pushed toward increasingly rigid interpretations of the Bible. The latter group went in the direction of acceptance of higher criticism and doubt about the miraculous.

In America by the turn of the century the Fundamentalist movement became theologically defined in terms of specific beliefs, and it had grown large enough to have the financial resources to focus upon evolution. The Fundamentalists found an ally against evolution in the political Progressive movement. By the 1890s it became apparent to many American political Progressives that Social Darwinism had become a rationalization for many of the social and political abuses that the Progressives sought to alleviate.[12] Their opposition to Social Darwinism was easily combined with the Fundamentalist campaign against scientific Darwinism.

Darwinism and Social Darwinism

The involvement of Darwinism in politics was a result of the confusion of Social Darwinism and scientific Darwinism in the public perception. As a consequence, the primary issue became academic freedom, because the campaign against Social Darwinism contributed[13] to the suppression of the teaching of scientific Darwinism. On the one hand, high school and college teachers desired to teach what was the nearly unanimous understanding of the scientific community concerning the origin of life and the human race. On the other hand, parents sought to control the education of their own children and perceived Darwinism as a threat to their well-being. Parents believed that historically the right to control education was built into the political structure of American life—this was founded on the local financing and control of the schools through local property taxes and local school board control of teachers, texts and curriculum.

The struggle to control the educational process passed through several definable stages. The first was the birth of evolution as a scientific idea from 1859 to about 1920. The second was a period of strength for the forces of political anti-evolutionism from 1920 to 1957. With the concern caused by the first artificial satellite, Sputnik, the struggle entered a period of increase for evolution as an educational and explanatory tool (1957-1980). The final stage can best be described as the rise of controversy, polemical dispute and an impasse in public opinion (1980 to the present).

Contrary to what some current Creationists claim, Darwin's work tended to stimulate the sciences in the United States rather than retard them. Darwin carried the day in the scientific community despite the known weaknesses of his theory, the paucity of the fossil record, and the limited nature of examples of transition. He succeeded on the basis that his thesis gave the most comprehensive explanation for the way nature worked, whether God was involved with it or not. The scientific success of Darwinism thus confronted religious and social resistance, which will be considered in the next chapter.

The Social and Political Implications of Creationism

The Components of Darwinism

One of the most significant developments surrounding Darwinism in the last century was its application to other disciplines by financiers, sociologists, political scientists and historians. The four most strategic components of Darwinism were as follows:

1) Population excedes what the environment can support. Darwin had adapted this point from the population analyses of Thomas Robert Malthus, interpreting it to imply that population normally tends to outstrip resources.[1]

2) There are random variations in the population.

3) In the struggle for existence, advantageous differences allow their possessors to survive.

4) Survivors transmit their advantages by heredity.

The second and fourth of these elements held no interest for financiers and sociologists, but the third interested them greatly.

The Adoption of Darwinism

In the hands of the sociologists, the natural struggle for existence became known as competitive individualism. To acquire the limited material resources of the planet, humans individually compete for access and control of those resources. Social progress was presumed to result from unfettered competition, unrestricted by law—a sort of war of all against all, which builds strength. The most beneficial results for the human race, and for individual justice, come about when the strong members of a society accumulate power and wealth and then use that wealth wisely. Life is a battle, with enlightened self-interest as the guiding principle.

Herbert Spencer, English philosopher and leading philosophical architect of Social Darwinism, coined the phrase "survival of the fittest" to express his perception of the battle to control scarce resources. This was a social concept, not a biological one, which was more oriented toward change than survival.[2] Social Darwinism permeated many aspects of American life in the last decades of the nineteenth century, but none so clearly and quickly as the business community. When Spencer died in 1903, at a time when ten thousand copies constituted a best seller, over 238,000 copies of his works had been sold. Social Darwinism was a congenial justification for the fierce business competition that saw monopolistic practices carried to the utmost, competition eliminated, and a few industrialists rise to a peak of power that was far greater than that of government or labor. The exploitation of wage earners through long hours, lack of protection from health hazards, summary dismissal without cause, and pay rates lower than subsistence were simply part of the whole picture. Spencer believed that change was naturally slow, and revolution was against the natural order, an order that included class structure. The Social Darwinists argued on the basis of this idea that misguided attempts by reformers to alleviate the conditions of the working class would not strengthen the poor.

Social Darwinism

Thus the elements of Social Darwinism, applied to business, affirmed that

> 1) business was controlled by a natural aristocracy, the winners over the weak in competition;
>
> 2) politicians were not subject to natural selection and therefore were not to be trusted;
>
> 3) the state should only protect property and maintain order;
>
> 4) slums and poverty were unfortunate but inevitable;
>
> 5) stewardship of wealth required addressing only true social injustice, very narrowly defined.

Following the implications of Social Darwinism, some employers practiced brutal and unconscionable abuse of the employee, the environment, and the power that came their way. Many others of the leaders of industry combined their Social Darwinism with selected passages from the Bible, seeking justification of their actions. This philosophy, combined with the Protestant tenet that each person should interpret the Scriptures independently without recourse to the guidance of priest or scholar, created a powerful tendency among the industrialists to promote education. They believed that education was the means by which the deserving poor might gain the insight and obtain the opportunity to begin their own climb to the top. Thus, Andrew Carnegie provided the funds to build literally hundreds of libraries across the country. In his own words,

"This, then, is held to be the duty of the man of wealth: To set an example of modest unostentatious living,... to consider all surplus revenues which come to him simply as trust funds, which he is called upon to administer, and strictly bound as a matter of duty to administer in the manner which, in his judgment is best calculated to produce the most beneficial results for the community—the man of wealth thus becoming the mere trustee and agent for his poorer brethren, bringing to their service his superior wisdom, experience, and ability to administer, doing better for them than they would or could for themselves."[3]

The leaders in the intellectual justification of Social Darwinism were the historian John Fiske and, more importantly, the sociologist William Graham Sumner. Sumner wrote,

"What matters it then that some millionaires are idle, or silly, or vulgar.... The millionaires are a product of natural selection, acting on the whole body of men to pick out those who can meet the requirement of certain work to be done.... They get high wages and live in luxury, but the bargain is a good one for society."[4]

Sumner argued that liberty, inequality and survival of the fittest, not liberty, equality and survival of the disadvantaged was the foundation of social progress. He explicitly opposed Jesus' teaching concerning the blessing that the "poor in spirit" may expect to receive. He also believed that Jesus' ministry among the disinherited in his day was misguided, and rejected the teaching of the parable about how difficult it is for the rich man to enter heaven.

Social Darwinism thus revived the old political theory of the divine right of kings, with the captains of industry replacing the political kings. The new leadership was based upon never-ending technological progress and scientific "proof" for its assertions in Darwinian evolution.

Opposition to Social Darwinism

While many of the churches that served the upper classes were influenced by Social Darwinism, much of the resistance to it also came from the religious community. Many of the Progressive political figures who attacked the excesses of Social Darwinism were religious. The obvious example is William Jennings Bryan, a highly visible three-time Democratic presidential candidate, Progressive politician, and world class orator, perhaps equalled in oratory in the late nineteenth century only by Robert Ingersoll. Bryan, a committed Fundamentalist, will be considered more closely in the context of the Scopes trial, but it is important here to note that his positions were compatible with those opposed to the Social Darwinists.

The intellectual challenge to Social Darwinism was led by another sociologist, Lester Frank Ward. Ward and others saw that "survival of the fittest" could be applied to nations, leading to imperialism and militarism. Combined with the hero cult, this ideology also contributed to talk of the super race and, ultimately, dictatorship. In his effort to ameliorate the worst implications of Social Darwinism, Ward took pains to build a case for a difference between animal economics and human economics. The advantage that man has is intelligence over instinct. Whereas Nathaniel Southgate Shaler, the Harvard geologist, blurred this distinction in his many popular books, finding all the types of human intelligence in the animals (just at a lower level), Ward sought to draw the distinction sharply and clearly. Man, Ward believed, should substitute rational choice for natural selection, because natural selection was terribly wasteful. Rational choice would be more efficient, and efficiency was a widely accepted social standard of the age for both sides in the debate. Ward also argued that unrestrained competition was actually in opposition to the survival of the fittest, since it frequently led to no competition, with shoddy goods driving out quality in the marketplace.[5]

The consequence of two decades of dominance by Social Darwinism was the building of strong religious, social and political resistance. Anti-evolutionism was born in this environment as a comprehensible reaction to Social Darwinism. It must be noted that the anti-evolutionists consistently confused biological Darwinism with Social Darwinism and rejected the former with the latter. That tendency to find evil social implications in a biological theory continues to the present.

The Church, Social Darwinism and Evolution

As already indicated, the Christian response to Darwinism varied a great deal. Christians were faced with a "...crisis of belief in creation, providence and design...," to which they responded in widely different fashions.[6] Philosophical deists and contemporary Unitarians had little difficulty adopting biological evolution. They perceived God as impersonal and remote, and they saw no reason to dispute restricting God to a role of Prime Mover or Original

Source. Biological evolution merely demonstrated the effectual means of God accomplishing his ends in the universe.

In the late nineteenth century the Catholic Church was much more ethnically oriented than now and was busy trying to assimilate the immigrating masses in the great developing urban areas of the United States.[7] For the Catholics, the doctrinal issues were other than creation, and there was less interest in or resistance to evolution. Evolutionary concepts found their way slowly, but without much controversy, into the books that were used in the Catholic schools.[8]

The controversy over evolution, therefore, was largely a Protestant affair. Within the Protestant community there was a wide divergence of opinion as well. Some pastors with wealthy congregations seemed to form an alliance with Social Darwinism, and while Darwinism seldom was featured in their sermons, it was clear from occasional references that they accepted both the social and the biological versions. The vast mainstream of American Protestantism in the last third of the nineteenth century, both the liberal and the conservative pastors and parishioners, adopted some form of theistic evolution as the most probable means of the creation of the universe.[9] Theistic evolutionists accepted that the creative purposes and methods of God are expressed in the Bible, but the process of creation is revealed by scientific research and includes evolutionary explanation. As Galileo had declared three centuries earlier, they agreed "that the intention of the Holy Ghost is to teach us how one goes to heaven, not how the heaven goes."[10]

Nevertheless, from the beginning there was a sizable Christian minority which found the consequences of Darwinism in its social forms so evil that they were forced to look at the roots of Social Darwinism in biological Darwinism and challenge that as well. The tendency toward materialistic and mechanistic views of the world, in the opinion of these observers, could only lead to moral decay and atheism.[11]

An early and frequent question concerned Darwin's own religious beliefs. He hated controversy, so he was not candid concerning his theology in his writings until his autobiography, which was not published until after his death. This fact is not surprising, since most of his writings were purely scientific. The most obvious opportunity was in The Descent of Man, but even there he chose to avoid controversy and remain relatively silent. When Francis Darwin, his son, edited the autobiography, he softened the antagonism toward the Bible at the request of Darwin's wife and daughter. Even so, it is clear that after his voyage around the world Darwin progressively doubted the historicity and authenticity of the Bible. He found Genesis and the miracles of Jesus most offensive. By the time of his death, he appears to have reached a point of agnosticism concerning the existence of God and the afterlife.[12] His personal view would be basically irrelevant save that some creationists presume that it is impossible to arrive at any other moral and religious perception than Darwin's if one accepts his science.

Of more significance than Darwin's perception of religion is the position of those who, for whatever personal motivation, found Darwinism a convenient tool for attacking the validity of the Bible. Huxley loved Darwinism for its "...complete and irreconcilable antagonism to that vigorous and consistent enemy of the highest intellectual, moral and social life of mankind—the Catholic Church."[13] Some other scientists joined Huxley, but most perceived Darwinism as a means of creation and retained their theological and metaphysical presuppositions.

Science Turned into Politics

What Darwinism appeared to do at the turn of the century was focus and clarify the divisions in an already troubled Christian community. The process of secularization was going on before Darwinism. Darwinism, along with German biblical criticism and the social gospel movement, simply increased the tension, forced a decision, and caused a sizable minority of Christians to be pushed toward a more literal interpretation of the Bible and a rejection of the science which they presumed had caused it.

The perception among the rising Fundamentalist minority that Darwinism constituted a major cause of unbelief was again based upon the activities of Herbert Spencer. Spencer sought to use Darwinism to build an ethic that would be independent of what he regarded as the discredited dogmas of religion. He essentially sought to build a combination of Darwinism and utilitarianism that would cause people to seek the highest common good allied with self-interest or personal happiness. As with most of Spencer's other theories, his contemporaries found basic inconsistencies between the mild form of hedonism he advocated and the common good. It was too optimistic a view of human nature. Further, most thinkers could find little foundation for the concept of conscience in a natural order that seemed bloodthirsty, unpredictable, and wasteful of life. His popularity was sufficient, however, for him to influence scientists toward a non-religious ethic and to awaken fear among the Fundamentalists.

For the Fundamentalists the particular issue that crystallized their opposition to evolution was a desire to protect children from evolution until they could understand its ethical implications, even if they accepted the scientific conclusions. Thus, concern was expressed over the content of school books, the teaching of evolution in the public schools, and the evil influence of evolution on moral behavior in society at large. These would become the issues of the twenty-five years leading up to the Scopes trial.

In 1900 evolution was nearly unanimously accepted within the scientific community as a theory of great validity, with explanatory and organizing power. Social Darwinism, which borrowed a portion of scientific Darwinism and applied it to economics, was fading in popularity. Politically, the Progressive reform movement was gaining strength that would peak within the next fifteen years under Roosevelt, Taft and a host of other reformers. Largely parallel in time with the Progressive movement, and allied in opposition to Social Darwinism, the Fundamentalist movement was also growing in the cities, the South and the Midwest.

As a movement, Fundamentalism was a religious reaction to the extensive change in American life in the late nineteenth century and the first decade of the twentieth century. A vast flood of immigration greatly increased the Catholic percentage of the population. A large-scale movement transferred workers from the farm to the city, with resultant crowded slums and a deterioration of old agrarian ideals in the population at large. There were strong pressures to make religion private, that is, to remove it from public life and to cultivate the soul in the private enclaves of the local church, which was increasingly removed from the public arena. As George M. Marsden suggests, the Fundamentalists experienced profound ambivalence toward the surrounding culture. These American Christians also underwent a dramatic transformation in their relationship to the culture. Respectable "Evangelicals" in the 1890s, they had become a laughingstock by the 1920s, ideological strangers in their own land.[14] Laughingstock they may have been, but they had not lost all political power. In the terms of the Fundamentalists, it was a war between naturalistic rationalism and supernaturalism for control of the churches.

In the three years from 1910 to 1912 a series of twelve booklets was published outlining the Christian faith, entitled *The Fundamentals: A Testimony to the Truth*. The fundamentals included

(1) the inspiration and inerrancy of the Scriptures;

(2) the Trinity;

(3) the deity and virgin birth of Christ;

(4) the special creation and the Fall of Man;

(5) the substitutionary atonement;

(6) the bodily resurrection and ascension of Christ;

(7) the personal, imminent and premillenial return of Christ;

(8) the regeneration of believers through Christ; and

(9) the bodily resurrection of Mankind to everlasting blessedness or everlasting conscious punishment.

The impact of these books upon American life was somewhat reduced by the intrusion of World War I, when society was mobilized to fight evils without rather than evils within. With the end of the war in 1918, however, the opportunity to return to the concern over modernism led to the formation of the World Christian Fundamentals Association. When William Bell Riley called a conference of concerned Christians in Philadelphia, over 6,000 persons gathered to form the WCFA and to elect Riley as president, a position he held until 1930, the period of the movement's greatest strength. Over the years, Riley organized mass meetings across the United States to promote the agenda and concerns of the Fundamentalists.

The original Fundamentalist publications were ambivalent toward evolution.[15] Evolution, theistically conceived, was an allowable option in the contributions of G. Frederick Wright and James Orr. However, Henry H. Beach and an anonymous contributor attacked Darwinism strongly as an unacceptable Christian alternative. The combination of evolution's threat to Man's unique place in the universe, the evil consequences of Social Darwinism, and the leadership of William Jennings Bryan, John Roach Stratton, William Bell Riley, William Brenton Greene, George McCready Price and Harry Rimmer were sufficient to turn the tide after the war.

William Jennings Bryan, leading Progressive politician, famed promoter of reform movements, and dedicated Baptist Fundamentalist, was uniquely qualified to lead the anti-evolution crusade. Bryan's most famous speech at the 1896 Democratic convention, "The Cross of Gold," initiated a large-scale movement to change the monetary system. His resignation from Wilson's cabinet as Secretary of State demonstrated his commitment to principle and to peace. Bryan was an ardent promoter of women's suffrage. And, not insignificantly for the anti-evolution crusade, he was concerned about children.[16]

Prior to taking up opposition to evolution, Bryan had promoted compulsory school attendance. He advocated expanding access to public secondary education and access to college education for the poor. In addition to promoting child labor laws, he also advocated a separate juvenile justice system, the building of playgrounds and parks with public monies, industrial continuing education for those working at a young age, homes for unwed mothers and foster homes for orphans so they did not have to live in the streets of the urban areas. Bryan was not a religious phony, out of touch with the needs of society; he was a battle-scarred old veteran of numerous political wars that were aimed at the preservation of the quality of life and the enhancing of human dignity.

The roots of that commitment grew, however, from his Christian faith. That is why modern scientists and historians looking back find his two presently unpopular causes, prohibition and anti-evolutionism, reprehensible. The effect of alcohol upon the lives of the poor then was more apparent than are the effects of alcohol upon the middle class in our own day. Is is therefore hard for us to see how a majority of the people in three-fourths of the states could pass statutes prohibiting the sale and distribution of alcohol. There is no need here to defend that stand, but there is need to note that it was not out of character for a movement committed to intervention to ameliorate the worst excesses of the society. The same may be said about Bryan and evolution.

After the war there was a new skepticism about the fruits of evolutionary progress, and an environment developed that was less conciliatory toward organic evolution as well. William Riley also focused attention on the threat that evolution posed to the theory of Man's origin and the disbelief in the Genesis account that could result from acceptance of evolution. Influenced by Riley, Bryan changed his own plan and developed two new speeches that took evolution to task.

Bryan's first attack was the speech, "The Menace of Darwinism," delivered in early 1921 and repeated at Bible conferences and Chautauqua summer conferences for the remaining five years of his life. The second and possibly more damaging speech was "The Bible and Its Enemies." In this speech Bryan found evolution to be the lurking philosophical foundation for many of the anti-biblical movements of the day, despite the fact that many of the ideas in the movement antedated evolution. In these speeches, Darwinism was characterized as unscientific and unconvincing. Bryan sustained his attack in 1923 in a widely-read article that contained his most sweeping assertion about evolution, and yet his most obviously absurd exaggeration of its importance. He claimed, "The evolutionary hypothesis is the only thing that has seriously menaced religion since the birth of Christ; and it menaces ... civilization as well as religion."[17]

Bryan promoted the idea that the word "theory" as used by a scientist means uncertainty. In reality, in the scientific community, an hypothesis is not a theory until the end of the testing process, when it has been established as certainly as is possible using the scientific method.[18] While Bryan accurately recognized that Darwin was not Baconian, that is, intending only to organize or classify the facts, he was out of touch with the nature of modern science.

Bryan's two speeches bequeathed a second attitude to subsequent Creationists—namely, that this scientific question ought not to be left in the hands of scientists who could not be trusted, but ought to be resolved in a popular forum. Bryan previously had similarly reasoned that the welfare of the working man could not be left in the hands of his employer, and that the welfare of the citizen could not be left in the hands of politicians beyond the control of voters. Bryan naturally expected the public forum to be the most appropriate arena to resolve the scientific dispute, despite its technical complexity.

Bryan's third legacy to the Creationist movement was continuing the confusion of organic evolution with Social Darwinism. He blamed Darwinism for the Great War. The doctrine of the "survival of the fittest" had been applied to the nations, and millions died as a result. Darwinism was a bloody doctrine in Bryan's semi-pacifistic eyes. Materialism seemed to Bryan to be the only possible outcome of Spencer's philosophy. Though Spencer was twenty years out of date, he served as a straw man to defeat in order to protect others from being drawn to materialism. Darwinism further encouraged the exploitation of labor by justifying selfish competition and implied that social change ought to come by slow evolution rather than by political reform or spiritual regeneration.

In his speeches, Bryan proposed three reforms: no evolutionists in the pulpits of churches, no non-Fundamentalists in church-supported schools, and neutrality in the public schools. By neutrality, Bryan did not mean teaching both beliefs, as modern Creationists do. Since he regarded creation as a religious doctrine, he believed that to maintain neutrality neither one should be taught. Bryan put into practice his belief in January 1922 by testifying in support of a Kentucky bill sponsored by Baptist minister John Porter, which required that evolution not be taught in the public schools. The bill died in Kentucky, but it was promoted in New York and Minnesota the following year and in twenty states within ten years. Bryan's belief in majoritarian rule indicated that the taxpayers had the right to decide what would be taught in the schools.[19]

The first anti-evolution law was enacted in Oklahoma in 1923. Following extensive political maneuvering, the primary issue was who controlled the content of the education of children. In mostly rural Oklahoma, the Populist feelings against scientific elitism comfortably carried the day. Florida was the only other state to follow suit in 1923. Again, Bryan's influence was strategic. He had moved to Florida to semi-retirement. In deference to his great influence, the legislature easily passed the bill for which he lobbied.

In his support of the passage of the anti-evolution law in Oklahoma, Bryan in his correspondence with the sponsors and in his speeches called for neutrality in the schools. Since the Bible could not be taught in the schools under the establishment clause of the First Amendment, Bryan thought that Protestants should only ask the exclusion of evolutionary teaching on the basis that it opposed Christianity. The issue was protecting the religious views of children from attack in the classroom. Since this was a matter of conscience, Bryan thought there should be no penalties attached.

So far, the campaign exhibited Bryan's limited objectives. The Florida legislation expressly stated that evolution should not be taught because creation could not be. Second, there was no penalty for disobedience, indicating, as he expressly stated, Bryan's wish not to interfere with anyone's right to believe evolution, just to prohibit teaching it to children. Bryan also did not seek to have evolutionary ideas completely removed from textbooks. The ideas and why they were thought to be true could be discussed, but they could only be presented as hypotheses, not as the truth.

Following the defeat of legislation in Tennessee in 1923, Bryan, Riley and others concentrated on that state in an effort to reverse the failure. In collaboration with a fellow Progressive, governor Austin Peay, Bryan's influence was sufficient to carry the day in Tennessee. Despite Bryan's opposition to penalties, the Tennessee legislature passed a law that called for small fines if teachers were convicted. It must be noted that Tennessee legislators also believed in Bryan's limited objectives because they later rejected a bill that would prevent school boards from hiring teachers who believed in evolution. They could believe the theory, they just could not teach it to children or teach it in a fashion that opposed Christianity.[20]

With this successful action in three states in 1923 and 1924, the stage was set for a legal showdown over whether the taxpayers and parents or even the states could control the curriculum of the public schools in detail. The entrenched opinion created an atmosphere in which the Scopes trial could occur.

The Scopes Trial

As a minority group within the Protestant churches, the Fundamentalists were growing in strength in the 1920s. While some historians presume they are a "Bible Belt" phenomenon, that is, from the South and Midwest, it is also true that a sizable percentage of Fundamentalists came from urban areas. Their colleges and conference centers, as well as conventions and offices, all tended to be in the cities, most of them in the Northeast.

The American Civil Liberties Union (ACLU) was the other major player in the Scopes Trial. The ACLU was founded during the first World War primarily to defend the rights of pacifists. After the war, its activities expanded to include all civil rights, although free speech became the most frequent cause. ACLU lawyers defended cases where Catholic schools were repressed in the South and Midwest by the Ku Klux Klan. The ACLU opposed the efforts of the American Legion to introduce required patriotic exercises in the classroom. It also supported cases opposing required religious instruction in which students were released from school to their churches or synagogues. Prior to the Scopes trial the ACLU had primarily defended those arrested for breaking a criminal law. As ACLU leaders observed the spread of anti-evolution laws, followed by either no penalties or no enforcement, they realized there were no defendants to represent. Feeling that the laws represented a potential threat that Fundamentalists could use at some future time, the ACLU decided to seek out someone to volunteer to be arrested in order to test the constitutionality of the law.

The ACLU selected Tennessee as the testing ground for its challenge to the anti-evolution laws. To find someone willing to take up the challenge, the organization advertised in the Chattanooga newspaper on May 4, 1925.[21] On the morning of May 5, after having seen the paper, a group of Dayton civic boosters led by George W. Rappelyea decided that this case would be just the thing to put their city on the map. They contacted one of the high school teachers, John T. Scopes, and asked if he would be willing to say he had taught evolution. Scopes had conducted a review using *Civic Biology*, an approved text that included some evolutionary content. On this rather inconsequential basis, Rappelyea and the others filed a complaint that afternoon against Scopes.

From this almost casual beginning, they were to succeed far beyond their wildest dreams in promoting Dayton to national prominence. Along with "*Brown v. The Board of Education of Topeka, Kansas*," the Scopes Trial became one of the most famous court cases of this century.

The ACLU indicated that by seeking to exclude evolutionary teaching for children, the anti-evolutionists were trying to enforce Christian orthodoxy in the public schools. This would not be the neutrality that the anti-evolutionists believed they were seeking. Based on its statement of objectives the ACLU had more in mind than just protecting freedom of speech. In presenting the case against the anti-evolutionists, the ACLU claimed that to "... inject ... propaganda in the interest of any particular theory of society to the exclusion of others should be opposed." On the other hand it promised to use "publicity," legal aid, test cases, and other means to "... service the friends of progress to a new social order...."[22] Thus, what was propaganda for the anti-evolutionists was publicity for the ACLU. A theory of family-oriented society with a personal, active God at its base was to be replaced by a new social order. To achieve these ends the ACLU needed to change public opinion, for which it intended to use the Scopes trial.

Opposition to the ACLU arose immediately from the newly formed (in 1924) World Christian Fundamentals Association. The stated goal of the WCFA in the Scopes Trial was the protection of traditional religious values shared by the majority of the residents of Tennessee. Both sides accused the other of using propaganda, and both were right. Under Tennessee's declaratory judgment law, Scopes could have requested a judgment on the constitutionality of the law without ever risking criminal prosecution.[23] Since that alternative would not have served the purposes of the boosters or the ACLU, it was never even considered.

The week the suit was filed, the WCFA was holding its national convention in Memphis. William B. Riley, the president, praised the Tennessee legislature for its courageous stance against the elitist establishment of the academic East. When Bryan, who also regarded evolutionists as an irresponsible oligarchy of self-styled intellectuals, spoke to the convention on Saturday, he was already aware of the warrant for Scopes' arrest, and he warned of an impending struggle. It soon became clear that the case would come to trial, and the WCFA asked if Bryan would be willing to join the prosecution. When he agreed, the Tennessee state attorney general appointed Bryan an unpaid special prosecutor. Bryan believed this was his great opportunity to alert Americans to the dangers of evolution.

Originally, the ACLU appears to have intended only to challenge the law as an infringement of academic freedom. However, when Bryan joined the prosecution, the ACLU expanded its objectives to include what it called the bigotry and intolerance that the anti-evolution crusade represented. This looked like an opportunity to bring down Bryan as well as the law. An all-star cast was assembled for the defense. The most famous personage was Clarence Darrow, a well-known criminal defense lawyer of the day and more than an intellectual match for Bryan. Like Bryan, he was a Democrat who had supported numerous Progressive causes. He had even spoken in support of Bryan's presidency in earlier elections, but they differed strenuously on religion.

A second member of the team was Dudley Field Malone. Malone had been Bryan's Third Assistant Secretary of State in the mid 'teens under Woodrow Wilson. Malone was a friend of Bryan, but again they differed strongly on the religious issue. Thirdly, the ACLU believed it had to have an in-house member on the team to keep things moving in accord with the ACLU's objectives. It sent Arthur Garfield Hayes, the ACLU's best-known civil rights lawyer. Finally, Charles Evans Hughes volunteered to argue the case before the Supreme Court if the case was appealed and proceeded that far. Hughes later sat on the Supreme Court.

A carnival atmosphere prevailed in Dayton. Booths were set up on the main street selling monkey trial souvenirs and food. Business boomed. Crowds came, including reporters by the hundreds. Some of the first live radio broadcasts emanated from Dayton. Finally, the newsreel cameras rolled, giving moviegoers a chance to see the happenings at Dayton. Both sides had plenty of opportunity to influence public opinion with interviews all around.

The Scopes trial lasted eight days. Popular opinion was on Bryan's side in the beginning. While the news reporting did change the minds of many people and Bryan was cast in a ridiculous light by the media, popular opinion was still with him at the end. Bryan actually exhibited more humor than Darrow and drew more favorable response from the gallery. As Bryan prepared for the case, however, he found that there would be serious difficulty in finding scientists to testify against evolution. The writings of one Oberlin professor opposed evolution, but Bryan found he had died five years before. George McCready Price, a Seventh-Day Adventist, seemed the best hope. Price was a self-taught geologist, and while he was a published author, he was not widely known or highly regarded for anything except his anti-evolutionary views. Price was in England, and since he could not attend, he advised Bryan to stick to the legal issues and avoid a head-on confrontation with the scientific community. Howard A. Kelly, a respected Johns Hopkins physician, reluctantly agreed to testify against the probabilities of at least human evolution, but he believed in the rest of evolution and pointed out that his position would undoubtedly come out in cross examination.[24] Samuel Untermeyer, who had just some months before represented the ACLU on a free speech case, stood with Bryan on the evolution issue. He urged Bryan to exclude all testimony by expert witnesses as irrelevant to the legal issue and weighted to the advantage of the other side. Thomas Stewart, the lead prosecutor for the state, heeded this advice and simply argued that the state which paid the bills had the right to control the content of public instruction. Stewart had the support of several Supreme Court cases.

Early in the trial Bryan concurred and decided that if the ACLU could be defeated on the narrow legal ground of state control of curriculum, the defeat would still appear to apply to evolution, helping the anti-evolution cause. Bryan and the prosecution succeeded in persuading the local judge to keep this narrow legal issue to the forefront. The ACLU defense lawyers sought to establish that the law infringed upon individual freedom of speech. The prosecution countered that the law did not proscribe individual personal belief in evolution or the freedom to espouse that view in either private conversation or public converse outside the classroom; the law only proscribed the right to teach evolution at taxpayers' expense. The right to free speech did not extend to the right to teach anything the teacher wished that opposed the law of the state or the established curriculum of the school board. With the jury excused from hearing this legal argument, the judge decided the constitutional issues on the basis of state and federal court decisions, concluding that the legislature had control over public education.

After repeated failures to turn the trial into a forum on evolution, Darrow finally began to impugn Bryan's intelligence. Essentially he appealed to Bryan's vanity by suggesting on the last day of the trial that Bryan take the stand as an expert witness on the Bible. Over the objections of Stewart and Untermeyer, Bryan agreed. Darrow thus sought to turn the trial into a forum on the Bible since he could not turn it into a forum on evolution. Darrow presented to Bryan a series of the standard biblical dilemmas:

> 1) How could Joshua make the day lengthen by making the sun stand still, when we know that the Earth revolves around the sun?
>
> 2) Did the flood destroy the fish? If not, did not this contradict the Biblical statement that all living creatures died except those on the ark? If so, where did the the fish come from?
>
> 3) Where did Cain get his wife?
>
> 4) Were the days of Genesis One 24-hour days?

Unfortunately for him, Bryan was trapped by his own literal approach to Biblical interpretation into an inconsistency, and he was made to look silly by the press. None of these questions applied to the legal issue, and they had no bearing on the case, but they did sway the opinion of history about the outcome of the trial. Almost buried under the newspaper publicity about Bryan's failure was the fact that Scopes was convicted and fined $100 by the judge. Bryan realized that he had major reconstruction to do, but he expected to be successful on the stump, as he had been before. However, when he suddenly died five days later in his sleep, the prime mover of the anti-evolution movement was gone.

The ACLU moved to pursue the appeal of the case to the Tennessee Supreme Court. The legal issue still remained academic freedom versus state authority over public school curriculum. Arguing that no person has the right to be employed by the state, and that it is the right of parents to control through their elected representatives the content of public instruction, the state prevailed on appeal. The state court then prevented an appeal to the U.S.

Supreme Court by reversing the conviction on the grounds that the judge rather than the jury set the punishment. At this point the prosecution withdrew the case, and there was, anticlimactically, nothing to appeal.

The consequences of the Scopes trial for the teaching of evolution and for the anti-evolution movement after 1925, however, were just beginning.

The Aftermath of Scopes, 1925-1957

There can be no doubt that the Scopes trial changed attitudes concerning anti-evolutionism for a significant portion of the American population. The liberal establishment's perception that anti-evolutionism was a rural Southern movement became a somewhat self-fulfilling prophecy, but the movement was not dead, as many members of the scientific community seemed content to believe. A second consequence was that a major shift in emphasis came about among textbook publishers, with evolution quietly shelved in the years after Scopes. Third, a rift developed between those Fundamentalists who were literalists and those who were not. The latter group developed into the post-World War II Evangelical movement headed by Billy Graham, Carl F.H. Henry and many others, evangelicals who renewed the effort to bring religion and science together. As a consequence of these divergent movements, the period from 1925 to 1957 was an extremely important period even though it is the most neglected by the historians of the Creationist movement.

Despite Scopes, the anti-evolution movement actually appeared to gain strength in the years that followed. At the time of Scopes, Oklahoma, Florida and Tennessee had anti-evolution laws. Scopes proved to the Fundamentalists that anti-evolution laws were not necessarily vulnerable to constitutional challenge. Just eight days after the end of the trial, a similar bill was introduced in Georgia. In 1926 three anti-evolution bills were introduced. The following year eighteen bills in fourteen states were introduced, the all-time high in legislative activity. During the decade of the 1920s, 37 anti-evolution bills in 20 states were introduced.[25] In most states these bills never got out of committee, but in Mississippi a bill similar to the Tennessee law was considered, although it went further by proscribing evolutionary textbooks and threatening dismissal for teachers who taught evolution.[26]

After the lengthiest debate of the legislative session, the bill passed both house and senate and was signed into law on March 11, 1926. The issues were clearly laid out in the debate. On the one side was concern for the freedom to teach what was believed to be the most accurate and best science available. On the other side was the right of parents through their representatives to control what was taught in the public schools, especially if it was regarded as an infringement of their right to religious freedom. The latter side was more frequently presented in terms of protection of children, not from science, but from a philosophy of materialism and antireligion. In part, this shift represents a continued confusing of biological evolution with Social Darwinism.

In 1928 the Arkansas legislature turned down an anti-evolution law. Then under the leadership of the editors of denominational magazines, the Missionary Baptists and Southern Baptists combined to mount an initiative campaign that successfully put a statute on the ballot in November 1928.[27] With opponents appealing to the electorate to avoid being the laughingstock of the nation and supporters quietly urging citizens to vote to protect the children, the initiative passed by more than a two-thirds majority. By this time it was clear that the media and the more urban states were going to reject such bills, and only the Southern rural states were likely to consider them. The Arkansas campaign was to be the last successful statewide anti-evolution campaign.

At this point the anti-evolutionists simply changed strategies. They discovered that local boards of education could be more easily influenced than entire states. The numbers were smaller, and the publicity was more subdued. As early as 1924 the State Board of Education in California had directed teachers to present evolution as a theory only, by which they meant a hypothesis, on the basis that evolution was subversive to Christianity.[28] Similarly, in 1924, before the Scopes trial, the North Carolina Board of Education, at the request of Governor Cameron Morrison, removed from approved textbook lists those that presented the origin of the human race in a fashion that disputed the biblical account. A few months after Scopes, the Texas Textbook Commission, under pressure from the governor, Miriam "Ma" Ferguson, ordered the removal of evolution from the textbooks used in that state. Louisiana followed suit in 1926.[29] When, however, no further state boards seemed willing to take action, this activity moved primarily to the local level. Pressure caused many school boards to purchase textbooks that avoided evolution altogether or spoke of "development" in its place. Some publishers even began issuing two editions of their texts to satisfy both sides in the controversy.

After failing to find a teacher to test the laws in Tenessee, Arkansas or Mississippi, the ACLU lost interest. By 1932 the ACLU had dropped the evolution legislation from its active roster of issues. This decision was aided by state attorney generals who refused to prosecute, teachers who ignored evolution and textbooks that avoided direct presentation of evolutionary concepts. Efforts to repeal the statutes repeatedly failed.

Only with difficulty may an assessment be made of exactly what happened in the textbook publishing business, since no comprehensive study of biology textbooks from the 1920s to the 1960s has been conducted. Legislative efforts faded during the Depression as economic survival became the overriding issue. The Fundamentalists were also absorbed in the effort to save the Prohibition (Eighteenth) Amendment to the Constitution and thus were distracted from the evolutionary issue. To produce textbooks that would sell to the broadest possible spectrum of buyers, textbook publishers simply eliminated mention of evolution from their texts. In the one limited study of textbooks to 1960, the authors found that new books issued in the late 1920s did not mention evolution.[30] Older textbooks, as they were revised, deleted Darwin and evolution from the text or from the index. Classification (taxonomy) rather than biological change became the focus of biological teaching.

Other evidence supports a general trend toward ignoring evolution. In 1930, Maynard Shipley, a partisan science popularizer, claimed that strong pressures were being exerted by the Fundamentalists upon authors and textbooks. The deletion of most references to Darwin and the total revision of the six pages on evolution in Hunter's *Civic Biology* was a prime example. Shipley believed that 70 percent of all teachers omitted all mention of evolution from the teaching of biology.[31] In 1932 Columbia University professors analyzed thirteen biology textbooks and found that only two presented the evolutionary connection of heredity and environment. Only one presented any theory of the origin of life.[32] In 1979 Gerald Skoog published a quantitative study showing that from 1930 to 1959 only three percent of the words in representative textbooks dealt with evolutionary topics, compared with eight percent for books published in the 1960s after the study of evolution was revived.[33]

College professors largely abandoned high school biology textbook writing during this period. From 1925 to 1960 apparently only two professional biologists wrote high school textbooks in biology. Hunter, author of one of the most controversial texts, attributed the lack of collegiate authors to the fact that biology was a hybrid of two sciences, botany and zoology, designed by educators rather than the scientific community.[34] Even if scientists had participated, the situation would not have changed dramatically because of the strong anti-evolution bias of the Fundamentalist community. Willard B. Gatewood, Jr. suggests that college professors assumed that the scientific community had won in the 1920s and simply did not know what had happened to high school biology.[35]

High school teachers, however, knew what was happening in a very personal way. Their academic freedom to teach evolution as a scientific theory was abridged in many states. In a few states, their right to believe in evolution and to be employed was questioned, even if they did not teach evolution. Thus, teachers learned to avoid evolution to protect their jobs. Communities all across the country required that evolution not be taught in their schools because it offended the religion of the students. One of the more extreme positions was that of Springfield, Kentucky, which eliminated biology and geology from the high school curriculum because the subjects could not be taught without evolution as a framework.[36]

The next step after eliminating the teaching of evolution was to eliminate belief in it. Many counties across the country, like DeKalb and Carroll counties in Tennessee, resolved not to hire teachers who believed in evolution whether they taught the theory or not.[37] Another problem arose for those already employed who believed in evolution. Paducah, Kentucky, approached this problem by refusing to rehire the sister of John T. Scopes, Lela V. Scopes, a mathematics teacher in that system. The Board further released biology teacher Esther Smith and English chair Aimee Buchanan for having discussed evolution in their classes. They were eventually reinstated, however, when no student could be found who would testify against them.[38] In 1942 a nationwide survey was conducted quizzing high school biology teachers concerning their treatment of evolution. Fewer than 50 percent taught anything about organic evolution in their classes, either positive or negative. Since the foundation of the position against evolution was that it offended the Christian faith of the students, school boards came rather close to using a test of religion for public employees.

While the focus of activities was on the high school level, college professors as well were not immune to dismissal from colleges with a strong Christian commitment if they taught evolution. Such actions were not new to the 1920s and 1930s, for Alexander Winchell had been dismissed from Methodist-controlled Vanderbilt University in 1878 for teaching that humans preceded Adam and that not all of them were descendants of Adam.[39] Similarly, in 1887, James Woodrow, uncle of President Woodrow Wilson, was dismissed from his position at Columbia Presbyterian Seminary and was tried before the Presbyterian General Council for accepting and teaching evolution, among other irregularities.[40]

Ralph G. Demaree, a professor of physics, was suspended in April 1923 at Kentucky Wesleyan College because of a public address in which he criticized Bryan, persons who attempted to prevent the discussion and teaching of evolution, and those who claimed science could not be reconciled with the Bible. He was reinstated only after he apologized, and agreed to refrain from official discussion of evolution.[41] Jesse W. Sparks was dismissed from the University of Tennessee, not even a church-affiliated school, for recommending to his students a text that treated human evolution favorably. Following support of Sparks by the American Association of University Professors (AAUP) for having academic freedom to teach a necessary topic, the University dismissed five additional professors for supporting him.[42] Finally, in May of 1926, A.L. Pickens, chair of the biology department at Furman College in South Carolina, was "constrained" to resign because his views of evolution opposed those of that Baptist institution.[43] While such actions were not widespread, they were sufficient to cause college professors in Fundamentalist-dominated states or schools to be cautious.

In the face of the occasional confrontation, many scientists adopted a military metaphor of medieval religion versus modern science. While this metaphor is historically inaccurate in that anti-evolutionism is mainly an American phenomenon of recent origin, the perception was accurate that modern science was not being taught in the schools. The limited political activity of biology teachers was too insignificant to influence the state of affairs until the launching of the artificial satellite Sputnik in 1957.

Thus, despite the public opinion losses at Dayton, the Funda-mentalists were largely successful in eliminating evolution from the public schools for thirty years. This closer look at the textbook campaign demonstrates that anti-evolutionism was not nearly as weak or defeated as the press and the scientists wished to believe. While the Fundamentalists assumed power in none of the mainline denominations, with the possible exception of the Missouri Synod Lutherans, their power remained strong as a significant minority in the United States. Splitting away into smaller but growing denominations and into associations of independent churches, they formed their own organizations, periodicals and publishing houses, but were largely ignored by the population at large.[44] They founded new Bible schools and colleges, which, allied with older Fundamentalist schools, graduated an increasingly educated and growing constituency. The new constituency was urban, middle-class and technologically oriented. This development is the most strategic of all because it provided a totally different type of available leadership pool for the renewed conflict of the 1960s. As one historian notes, "... they were citizens of means and influence in local communities."[45]

The movement also branched into broadcasting and film. The developments in radio and television are well known, with the anti-evolutionism of Jerry Falwell and James Kennedy culminat-ing thirty years of development in this field. Film efforts are less well known, but the "Sermons from Science" series of Irwin A. Moon under the auspices of the Moody Institute of Science were immensely popular in the 1950s.

Some other strands of the anti-evolution movement also persisted. With George McCready Price's influence still strong, the Seventh Day Adventists continued to write against evolution, but as they retreated into their own elementary schools, their influence on public education began to decline. The Jehovah's Witnesses mentioned evolution as a great evil in nearly every issue of their weekly magazines, but their numbers and influence remained isolated and relatively small.

Throughout this period, there continued to be those who viewed the relationship of science and religion as one of contention. The best known author of nearly two dozen books in the 1930s from the Creationist side was Harry Rimmer, a Presbyterian evangelist. Rimmer must be differentiated from modern Creationists since he granted the great age of the Earth, although his arguments against evolution have been frequently borrowed by later Creationists. Arthur I. Brown, a physician turned evangelist, also wrote extensively in the 1930s and 1940s against evolution. Perhaps most remarkable of all was Frank Lewis Marsh, who earned a Ph.D. in plant ecology at the University of Nebraska. He wrote *Evolution, Creation and Science*, which Willard Gatewood refers to as "... one of the most sophisticated anti-evolutionist works in existence."[46] This book was taken so seriously that the well-known geneticist Theodosius Dobzhansky reviewed it. Dobzhansky was critical of the book but granted that it was the work of a "... reasonable and well-informed person."[47] The majority of the Christian community, who were willing to avoid combat with science, were somewhat embarrassed by the excesses of the Fundamentalists. More importantly, however, large numbers of Christians found no difficulty in interpreting Genesis in a non-literal sense and evolution in a non-atheistic sense and were willing to synthesize science and faith. The majority, however, was relatively silent.

During the 1930s and 1940s the philosophy of science and the history of science came to prominence within the academic community. The relationship of science and religion was much more fully explored during this time. The historic Protestant relationship to the scientific movement was analyzed, and philosophical points of tension and differences in definition were exhaustively catalogued. Little of this immense literature is read now, primarily because outside of Philosophy of Science departments at the few schools that have them, scientists have largely become ignorant of their own history and philosophy and are content simply to practice their discipline.[48] In this intellectual environment theistic evolution was for the most part ignored. As a consequence when the Creationists became powerful again there was little theistic evolutionary tradition to offset it. The non-Creationist conservative theology of Bernard Ramm is notable for its isolation during the quarter century from 1930 to 1955.

It must then be concluded that the thirty-year truce between the anti-evolutionists and the evolutionists was a period of importance for the gathering of resources for a new conflict that would erupt when the right event came along. That event was the launching of Sputnik by the U.S.S.R. in 1957.

Sputnik and the Renewed Battle Over Evolution

As we have noted, during the thirty-year period following the Scopes trial, anti-evolution laws were not enforced in the states where they existed because publishers essentially eliminated evolution from the textbooks. This relative tranquility was abruptly upset by the advent of Sputnik, the first satellite launched by Man. Within months dozens of newspaper and magazine articles raised the question of whether our educational system was effective in light of apparently superior Russian technological achievement. Naturally, the hardest look was taken at the sciences, and the feeling persisted that there were serious shortcomings in teaching methodology and content at the high school level.

Congress immediately authorized large increases in the budgets of NASA, the National Science Foundation (NSF) and the National Defense Student Loan Fund. The NSF was given a mandate to spend a portion of its new money on model science textbooks written by experts in the various fields who would draw upon the most recent research. As a consequence new textbooks were written in Physics, Chemistry, Mathematics and Biology. These were widely adopted following their promotion in summer study programs for bright high school students and summer seminars for high school teachers. None of the books were controversial except for the new biology series written by the Biological Sciences Curriculum Study (BSCS). Of the several versions of the

BSCS texts, one used evolutionary concepts as the unifying theme. With its exceptional list of contributing authors, the series gained wide acceptance and eventually accounted for half of all sales of biology textbooks in the 1960s.

A second major impetus to renewed controversy over evolution was the centennial of the publication of the *Origin of Species*, in 1959. Numerous publications, conferences, and symposia appeared that year which brought media attention to evolution and to its neglect in the schools. Perhaps the one event that crystallized Fundamentalist thinking was an address by Sir Julian Huxley on Thanksgiving Day entitled, "The Evolutionary Vision." In this speech, Huxley claimed there was no longer need nor room for the supernatural. Man, he said, could no longer find refuge in a self-created father figure divinity. His words supported the long-held view that evolution inevitably led to atheism.

As was the case in the early 1900s when the impact of evolution reached the popular audience, the reaction began. Fundamentalist Christians became concerned over the teaching of evolution to their children and also concerned over the effect upon society in general. Just as in the 1920s, they still believed that the natural outcome of evolutionary belief was anti-religious and morally debilitating. At approximately the same time a renewed effort to clarify issues within the Christian community was undertaken. The tendency to describe issues in either/or categories, allied with the viewpoint that evolution could be more easily defeated if there were no neutral ground, encouraged the Creationists to attack theistic evolutionists with renewed vigor.[49] Campaigning to remove any Christian support for the theists, Creationists argued that it was a delusion that Christianity and evolution could be compatible. This position was necessary in order to establish that there were only two alternatives, which in turn allowed Creationists to claim, as Henry M. Morris did, that "Any negative evidence against evolution is the same as positive evidence for creation."[50] Another position that some Creationists adopted was that Christians who accepted evolution were well-meaning but misguided. This position led to a separation in 1963 of the Creationists from the American Scientific Affiliation, because the Creationists regarded the theistic evolutionists as little different from agnostic evolutionists.

The third facet of the renewed campaign was to resolve the problem of evolution in the schools. With evolution so thoroughly entrenched among the scientific community, and with so little respectable authority from that community on their side, the Creationists abandoned Bryan's campaign to eliminate the teaching of evolution. To achieve equal treatment, they inverted Bryan's argument and attempted to secure equal time for Creationism by seeking to introduce "creation-science" into the public schools anywhere evolution was taught. Mistrust of science and the American sense of fairness gave the Creationists a broad and large support base. Encouragement came from other organizations such as Jerry Falwell's Moral Majority (now disbanded) and the writings of the popular Francis Schaeffer, who made "secular humanism" a household word.

Summary

The Creationists have gained a rather significant amount of attention in the modern American social structure. They have amassed a large following, with hundreds of thousands of Americans and numerous libraries on their mailing lists. Estimates of the numbers who consider themselves Creationists reach as high as 18 million, most of whom would also be within the group the press labels Evangelical Christians.

Creationists have found numerous school boards that would pass resolutions favorable to the presentation of Creationism in the classroom, and failing that they have created their own schools by the hundreds. Creationists have been instrumental in introducing (but not enacting) legislation in at least 35 states seeking to legalize the teaching of Creationism alongside evolution in the science classroom. In Arkansas and Louisiana they secured passage of such laws which were challenged in the courts and struck down. They have influenced textbook adoptions on a statewide basis in several states, especially Texas and California, although in California their power seems to be waning.

Their activity has attempted to convince Americans that fairness demands equal treatment of Creationism with evolution. Surveys indicate the magnitude of their success, but the public seems strangely unaware of the nature of what the Creationists really believe. They have also sought to convince Americans of the obverse—namely, the unfairness of their opponents. They dismiss Christians who disagree as the dupes of the evolutionists. They accuse the scientific community of relativism and closedmindedness. They accuse the courts of bias.

The major issue remains the validity of their position. There is no doubt concerning their sincerity and their desire to influence society positively. We cannot, however, equate sincerity with reasonableness, nor even with legitimate interpretation of the Bible. To make a meaningful decision about the validity of Creationism it is necessary to consider the scientific evidence, the hermeneutical evidence, and the consequences of Creationist political action.

Clearly, the Creationists have a long and complex history. They are subject to the same social environment and influences which influence their opponents. They represent an attempt to preserve the perceived best of the past in a fashion that appears to be inappropriate because it departs from traditional Christianity, seeks an impossible return to a simpler age, distorts the nature of the physical world and denies the past.

The Scientific Arguments of the Creationists

Having surveyed the main Creationists and what they believe, traced the history of the old anti-evolution crusade, and reviewed the beginnings of the new "equal time" crusade, we must now consider the particular arguments of the Creationists against the theory of evolution. Since evolutionary theory is an integral organizational principle for the biological sciences, it is essential to begin with biological arguments. This discussion, because of its limited objective of illustrating the conflict between scientists and Creationists, is not comprehensive. Many of the complex and technical matters are not considered here. More comprehensive surveys may be found in the books written by scientists about Creationism.[1]

The Problem of "Kinds"

The Creationists reject the factuality of biological evolution from simple organisms through increasingly complex forms. They reject the idea that this process has taken hundreds of millions of years and that the geological and biological evidence points in this direction. They believe that the Bible teaches a short life-span for the universe of perhaps 10,000 years, which does not allow sufficient time for evolution to have occurred. They also believe that it teaches that species are fixed and cannot evolve.

A starting point for many Creationists is the Genesis account, chapters one and two, which indicates that each animal or plant reproduces after its own "kind." Instead of interpreting these chapters as a description adequate to represent what is seen occurring about us in everyday life, the Creationists attempt to extrapolate it to a universal scientific principle that applies to all situations and across all time.

There is a problem with defining the biblical "kind." First, most Creationists do not wish to identify "kind" with species[2], for if there were evidence that evolution between species had occurred, it would imply that the "kinds" are not fixed. Frequently, but not uniformly, "kind" is identified with genus or family, in the ascending taxonomic order from specie to genus, family, order, class, phylum and kingdom. For example, the *Felidae* (cat) family, along with dogs, bears, otters, etc., make up the order of *Carnivora*. The *Carnivora*, along with the *Primates* and other orders, make the class *Mammalia*. The *Mammalia*, along with the *Aves* (birds), *Reptilia* and others, make up the phylum of *Chordata* (those animals with spinal columns). Beyond the phyla are the five kingdoms, of which the animals are one (*Metazoa*).

Duane T. Gish indicates that the genus *Canis* consisting of domestic dogs, coyotes, wolves, jackals, etc., make up a kind because they are interfertile (if forced) although the young may not be viable, which implies that interfertility is the criterion for "kind." In the case of the cats, however, it is not the genus *Felis* (small cats) but the family *Felidae* that Gish equates with the biblical "kind." *Felidae* includes the lions, tigers, cheetahs, lynx and others. In this case there is no mention of interfertility, but the differences are so great that biological taxonomy cannot be used to define "kind."[3] Definition in terms of interfertility alone proves unacceptable to Creationists, because several *Drosophila* (fruit fly) species developed in the laboratory are not interfertile. These cannot be considered different kinds by the Creationists since to do so would imply that evolution of one kind from another takes place. Therefore, Creationists adopt a meaning of kind which excludes taxonomy, interfertility and microbiological criteria, but which is based on morphological type, that is, those animals which have the same gross physical structure.[4]

Using morphology or structure to define "kind" raises additional difficulties for the Creationists. While interfertility can be forced in captivity for lions and tigers, for example, it does not normally occur in the wild. Lions and tigers are considered different species by biologists on the basis of what is called reproductive isolation; they do not mate naturally in the wild. Biologists accept the principle that common chromosomal material combined with reproductive isolation leads to the assumption that the species evolved at a particular time in the past from a common ancestor. Since the Creationist believes that forced interfertility establishes lions and tigers as the same "kind," what is to be done with the physical differences that enable scientists to always conclude to which species a living example, or even a skeleton, belongs? In this case the physical criterion that would lead to calling them different species must be ignored by the Creationists. The difficulty in classifying the lion and tiger indicates that the Creationist cannot use even the primary element of morphology consistently. The result is that the Creationist use of "kind" is useless for taxonomic or research purposes.

The Creationists largely ignore the developments of the last thirty years in the area of the genetic basis of evolution. Discovery of the genetic basis of evolution is the result of studies of proteins and nucleic acids (DNA and RNA) contained in living organisms. A key discovery was the establishment of the nucleotide base sequences in the DNA molecule. Scientists believe that infrequent, but cumulative changes take place in the DNA sequence, roughly about 2% per five million years. This is sufficient to account for evolution over 600 million years. The significance of the study of, for example, hemoglobin (one of the proteins), is that the divergence of different species can be quantified. The human and the gorilla differ by only a single amino acid on each of the two hemoglobin chains. Humans differ by 17 and 24 acids from cattle, implying an earlier divergence. This is significant primarily because it gives an independent verification of classical taxonomy based on interfertility and visible characteristics. It also gives a relative chronology of the divergence of species which can be checked against the traditional family trees of evolutionary theory.

The Creationists ignore this remarkable confirmation of taxonomy and divergence by focusing on a single issue: an attempt to prove that all genetic change is damaging, or that it is "horizontal" and not "vertical."[6] Biologists respond that even if only one change in a thousand is beneficial, it is sufficient for natural selection to work. They regard the Creationist claim that all genetic change is damaging as a falsehood.

Biologists reject the Creationist confusion in using "kinds" as a biological definition, since they regard the evidence for change as conclusive in very small living organisms. The most famous case is in Drosophilia experiments where the result was new non-interfertile species of fruit flies, some of which were blind. Biologists and geologists find additional evidence from organisms that have been isolated geographically from others of the same species and that have developed quite differently. An early example of this phenomenon which has been found many times since, was Darwin's famous finches from the Galapagos Islands that were both distinct morphologically and not interfertile with other finches. His conclusion that these birds constitute different species has subsequently been verified by more recent biologists.[7] The conclusion drawn by biologists about evolving species is an inference from these living examples and many other examples from the fossil record.

There are additional types of evidence for evolution to which the Creationists seldom refer. In addition to the protein and DNA studies mentioned above, much work has been done with homologous bone structure that biologists use as evidence of common ancestry. Such studies are extremely complicated and difficult. Few Creationists discuss these issues because of the in-depth understanding necessary and the difficulty of making them clear to a lay audience. Rather, the Creationists would insist that the scientists are wrong when they suggest that such discoveries are adequate to explain how mutation and the consequent natural selection take place.[8] Rather than successfully refuting such evidence, they frequently label it as inconclusive.

The Fossil Record

The second major challenge to traditional scientific interpretation involves the fossil record. Creationists deny the validity of the scientific dating of fossils, the scientific interpretation of what has been found, and the conclusion scientists have drawn—namely, that evolution has occurred.

The Creationists' major claim is that there are no links between species (transitional forms) to fill the gaps in the fossil record, an argument first proposed by Baron Cuvier, the French biologist, in the 1700s.[9] When confronted with fossils such as the Archaeopteryx which has both reptilian and birdlike characteristics, attempts are made to prove the fossils a forgery, or to deny that any of the characteristics are genuinely reptilian. Most recently the British astronomer Sir Fred Hoyle made such claims on the basis of new photographs. However, thorough investigation by eminent paleontologists of his claims that the fossil was double-struck by a forger have demonstrated that there were actually two layers of feathers on the original specimen rather than a forgery. A special case of the problem of gaps is the Creationist claim that there are no pre-Cambrian fossils preliminary to the sudden appearance of the complex Cambrian type. The evolutionists respond that there were no hard parts to fossilize and the lack of fossils is to be expected, although recently microbial pre-Cambrian fossils have been discovered.

Most evolutionists concede the gaps, while indicating that there are very clear reasons why the gaps occur. For example, soft parts do not preserve well; deposit takes place under rather restricted conditions;[10] the origin of new species is initially confined to a small geographic area and a relatively short time span, lessening the likelihood of deposits being preserved or discovered later. Only a minute proportion of all life forms are presumed to have been fossilized, and only a small fraction of that discovered.

Despite these problems, a vast number of transitional forms have been discovered in the past one hundred years linking the main types of vertebrates which have hard bones and teeth that fossilize. The transition from reptiles to early mammals is one of the clearest paleontological evidences for evolution. Biologists and paleontologists expect the gaps to continue to close, as they claim gaps have been doing over the last century. Scientists also, however, have become much more cautious about the "tree of life" diagrams popular in biology books of 30 to 70 years ago. Now the diagrams tend to resemble flowing streams, with the entry of certain fossil types at different stages, and the connectives left out. The reason is obvious, for antecedents or transitional forms for many life forms have simply not been found, especially soft-bodied invertebrates concerning which most evolutionists concede that connections are unknown. Still, the evidence found so far indicates that the evolutionist does not have to demonstrate every connection for evolution to be true.

Creationists, on the other hand, maintain that the gaps have remained fairly stable, despite the century of paleontological effort. They suggest that rather than filling the gaps in the fossil record, new discoveries simply expand our knowledge of life forms that have existed during the last 10,000 years. The newer theory of punctuated equilibrium is to the Creationists tacit admission that the gaps exist. Punctuated equilibrium assumes that the gaps represent periods of accelerated evolutionary change which occurred so rapidly that no geological record was left, followed by long periods of relative stability. The Creationists portray the scientific community as deeply divided on the reality of evolution. The division was real prior to the advent of genetics (circa 1900), but was practically non-existent from then until recently. The debate among scientists is over pace and method, not the concept of evolution itself. As long ago as 1927, however, Maynard Shipley noted that "...the clerical opponents of evolution, along with a few lay critics, would have the public believe that contemporary scientists are divided on the subject; or even that the theory of evolution has been abandoned by a large number number of American and European paleontologists, geologists, comparative anatomists, embryologists, anthropologists, sociologists, etc."[11] The issue then as now is the process, not the legitimacy of the theory among the scientists.

Punctuated equilibrium as a scientific theory is also in opposition to another claim of the Creationists, that biologists believe in a smooth, uniform development over time from simple creatures to complex ones. Punctuated equilibrium discounts this supposed smoothness, and most scientists deny adherence to smoothly-growing complexity. The complexity of organisms is difficult to compare. There is no measure of complexity. Even at the microbiological level which the Creationists ignore, the issue is not so much complexity as expansion of alternatives. The process is not clearly directional, but one of modification with subsequent natural selection.[12]

Scientists are absolutely clear that the fossil record traces a pattern of change over time. In other words, the record shows a factual basis for change from simple one-celled organisms to more complex ones, but not uniformly. This is why they so confidently call evolution a fact, although it is an inference. The processes of change are less clear, and this is the area for debate within the scientific community. The Creationists have taken the arguments over process as evidence of scientific doubt about the reality of evolution, blurring distinction between the "what" of evolution and the "how."

The Creationists clearly oppose the scientific interpretation of the evidence for change in life forms over time. Their presupposition is that change cannot occur, and that the evidence for change— so clear to biologists and geologists—must be rejected.

The Origin of Life

The Creationists reject scientific taxonomy as valid because it conflicts with their interpretation of the meaning of the Genesis "kinds." They reject the fossil and genetic evidence of change because there can be none if each kind begets its own forever. While these issues center primarily around interpretation, the next issue is whether it is physically possible for life to begin without God's direct and immediate intervention.

The Creationists say that there is no way to get from inert matter to living reproducing matter without the intervention of God. This is the "origin of life" problem. In the book *Scientific Creationism*, the issue is joined by stating that evolution predicts that the processes still operate today and that life should be coming from non-life today. Since we don't observe this happening, evolution must be modified with a secondary assumption that conditions were different on the primeval Earth.[13]

This presentation exhibits several of the methods that Creationists use when arguing against evolution. The first is to establish criteria for evolution that scientists themselves do not accept. Creationists claim initially that it is a "basic prediction" of evolution that the process of creating life from non-life is still occurring. However, such a prediction can be found in no evolutionary text from Darwin's day to the present. Rather, all the texts assert that the original planetary conditions were different and that the process is not going on at present. The Creationists appear to refute something in evolution that evolution does not claim.

The Creationist then proposes that the different primal conditions were a "secondary" assumption, that is, an afterthought brought in as a patch to save the theory. Actually, the primal conditions were simply not investigated until the 1920s because there were more pressing matters concerning taxonomy and the development of paleontology prior to that time. When the time was finally available, the assumptions about initial conditions were derived from the then-current assumptions about planetary atmospheres. While the cosmogony (theory of the origin) of the solar system has changed significantly since 1920, the assumptions about the original atmosphere have remained relatively stable. The study of the original atmosphere has been "good" science in that it can be tested against the cosmological theses.

The next step for the Creationists was to discount the experiments that have shown that organic molecules can indeed result from the infusion of energy into inorganic compounds. Duane Gish presents this argument in his pamphlet entitled "Summary of Scientific Evidence for Creation." Gish claims scientists have not even remotely approached the synthesis of life from nonlife. He further claims the laboratory conditions of the experiments are artificially imposed and extremely improbable. He concludes that life did not emerge by the process that evolutionists postulate.[14] Scientists agree that they have not yet synthesized life. The remoteness of that goal is apparent, in fact, more so now than twenty years ago, since the understanding of the complexity of this process has grown. However, Gish's statements disguise the issues. Of course the conditions are artificially imposed. Every scientific experiment imposes restrictions in some way in order to control the variables and produce interpretable results. Artificial conditions are a normal part of experimentation.

Gish's claim that these imposed conditions are "extremely improbable," ignores the fact that these conditions are the best that can be inferred from present cosmological theory. They are not improbable either to biologists who are doing the experiments or to the cosmologists who have developed a plausible explanation of the evolution of the earth's atmosphere from those primal conditions to the present, an explanation that is compatible with the concurrent developments upon the planet.[15] They are only improbable to Gish, who wants the evolutionists to be uniformitarian about the condition of the atmosphere, which they are not.

There are numerous additional problems with evolution that Creationists consider. While it is beyond the scope of this work to evaluate them all, they are considered and consistently refuted in the recent outpouring of books about Creationism by scientists.

Creationist Disputes with Geology, Astronomy and Physics

It is evident that Creationists have many problems with modern biology and paleontology and the use of evolutionary theory in those sciences. Even so, it is a surprising fact that Creationists reject not merely evolution, but also ideas and even matters of fact in all the sciences.[16] Creationism is not, at present, just anti-evolution; it is ultimately anti-scientific in its approach and its conclusions. This is not a new discovery, for it was recognized by Maynard Shipley, president of the Science League of America in 1927. He saw the campaign by the Fundamentalists as an attack upon geology, psychology, anthropology, sociology and history as well.[17]

The primary issue with both geology and physics is the various methods of dating geological formations and specific fossil-bearing rocks. The scientific community, with very near unanimity, agrees that a variety of differing methods point to great age for the universe and for this planet. While differing interpretations of the facts frequently lead to disputes that cause some estimates of the age of the universe to double others (ten to twenty billion years), none of the disagreements lead to a difference of 450,000 times other estimates, which would be the case if we accept the 10,000 year age of the Earth most Creationists regard as the upper limit.

Because most Creationists recognize that dating is their most vulnerable point, they have proposed several reasons why the universe appears old. The first is the suggestion that the universe was created by God "in motion," that is, with the appearance of great age. Although the stars were created at great distance, the light from them was also created in transit to the Earth. A second approach is simply to deny that there are any independent dating techniques that are reliable beyond 10,000 years. The third technique is to discount radiometric dating with challenges to the reliability of extrapolations back more than 10,000 years.

The proposal that the Earth was created with the appearance of great age occurred shortly after geologists first established a long pre-history in the 1830s. Nevertheless, it did not gain a significant following in the Christian community during a period of time when most Christians were determined to maintain compatibility between science and religion. This suggestion appeared again in the late nineteenth century in the writings of Philip H. Gosse, a devout naturalist. He proposed the "omphalos" theory that, "when the catastrophic act of creation took place, the world presented instantly the structural appearance of a planet in which life had long existed."[18]

The concept made a brief comeback in the 1920s during the time of the Scopes trial, but again it was largely rejected by Christians who believed that it implied that God was a deceiver, that he would be guilty of fooling Man, and that Man then could not trust the senses. Most Christians rejected this proposed solution as a subtle form of agnosticism about the reliability of the senses.

In recent years, as the Creationists have realized the importance of the astronomical evidence, the proposal of "apparent" great age has become more prominent. Henry Morris has clearly expressed it in his works, using it specifically as a means to refute the astronomical evidence for the great age of the universe. He considers it a part of the argument that the universe was created "mature," that is, when plants were created, soil was in place, light from the Sun was here, and that light from the stars was created *en route* from the stars that were more than 10,000 light years away.[19]

Again, most Christians have rejected this proposal for the old reason that it makes God a deceiver and for the newer reason that it is an *ad hoc* hypothesis to support a particular interpretation of the book of Genesis. This *ad hoc* proposal is not testable or refutable, fails to stimulate research, and is unlikely to advance scientific knowledge.

The second contention is that there is no reliable dating mechanism that reaches back more than 10,000 years. To check this contention, it is necessary to look at methods scientists use to date artifacts. Tree ring dating with living and dead bristlecone pines reaches back 8000 years, beyond the 6000 years of some Creationist chronologies. The study of plate tectonics and continental drift leads to the conclusion that the Western Hemisphere and Europe and Africa were once attached 200,000,000 years ago. The rate of drift is not assumed to be constant, as some Creationists claim, but the average rate of drift is approximately two centimeters per year. The present rate which can be measured is slightly above that. For this event to have occurred during the time frame the Creationists propose requires the continents to move apart at the rate of 200 meters per year on the average.[20]

The major issue for the Creationists, however, is the radiometric dating method (the use of radioactive isotope decay rates) which is used to date rocks and fossils. Henry Morris makes the remarkable claim in *Scientific Creationism* that rocks are not dated by radiometric methods, or even by the fossils in the rocks, but by what he calls "index fossils" alone.[21] These index fossils are carefully selected by evolutionary scientists to make the dating of rocks fit the evolutionary scheme.

It is unclear why Morris would claim that radiometry is not used to date rocks. The development of the geological column in the 1820s gave only relative comparisons of age. Initial estimates of the actual age of rocks were based upon rates of deposition, which, because they varied from place to place, gave inconsistent estimates. It was not until the advent of radiometric dating that geologists reached some stability in the dating of fossils. A survey of geological literature reveals that the radiometric method is used for dating rocks more than it is used for anything else, with the exception of carbon 14, which is used on human artifacts of the last 50,000 years. It is true that there are occasional anomalous results, as the Creationists claim, but unfortunately for their assertion, the anomalies are exceptions. On the other hand, nearly all of the dated samples coincide with the geological column, becoming an independent verification of the column that was developed before Darwinism was even on the scene.

Morris' other complaint against radiometric dating is that scientists inappropriately assume that the radioactive rocks existed in a closed system, that is, that no radioactive material has been added or removed since the beginning of time. A further inappropriate assumption, according to Morris, is that the rock when originally deposited could have contained none of the "daughter element," the end result of the decay process. His third claim of false assumptions is that the scientists assume a constant rate of decay over time. The last of these is the most testable and the one most vigorously defended by the scientists. They reason that a primary evidence for the stability of decay rates is that differing radioactive measurements give generally congruent results and are consistent with the astronomical measurements of time. Creationists find this reasoning less than convincing due to its inferential basis, which they equate with uncertainty.

The Creationists raise apparently serious difficulties, such as that free neutron capture would cause uranium methods to give dates that are too large, that decay rates may be variable, that 200-year-old basaltic lavas in Hawaii give potassium-argon ages of 160 million years or more, and other similar claims.

The Creationist idea of neutron capture is a special case of the argument that uranium is unreliable for measuring age because it does not exist in a "closed system." This means that we cannot be assured that none of the daughter element into which the radioactive uranium isotope decays was present when the process began millions of years ago. It is true that rigorously closed systems do not occur in nature. It is also true that some samples of uranium are unusuable for dating, but the contamination of these can normally be identified. Even so strong a critic (from within the scientific community) as Henry Faul says that many of the samples satisfy the "closed system" requirements well enough to be used for dating.[22]

The second argument, that decay rates may vary, is based upon several claims. One is that decay rates may be affected by cosmic rays. What is surprising is that this was refuted as long ago as 1928. Creationists have also suggested that the reversal of the Earth's magnetic field changes the decay rate. The Creationists cite no evidence for this and there is none. They also suggest that pressure, temperature and chemical state affect decay rates. Research to date has found no more than a 4% variation due to these causes, far short of the 4,500% factor needed to move from 4.5 billion to 10,000 years for the age of the Earth.

The anomalous basalt data from Hawaii was published in 1968 by John J. Naughton of the University of Hawaii. Naughton has pointed out that Morris misinterpreted his results, and that he gave the dates as evidence that the method could not be used with basalts that erupted in the deep ocean, due to excess argon in the environment of the magma chamber where the basalt originated. The use of the data is a serious distortion of the intent of the author.

Other thorough investigations of specific Creationist charges against radiometric dating reveal repeated misinterpretations of data and conclusions, and the use of outdated sources. The Creationists have yet to provide an interpretation of radiometric evidence that explains the results better than current scientific theory or that predicts new results that would be verifiable.

Astronomical Evidence

The biological and geological issues in this debate are complex and difficult for the non-specialist to master. The consequences of accepting the Creationist short age for the universe are clearer and easier to understand, however, when one considers the astronomical evidence.

The most significant non-geological and non-radiometric evidence for the age of the universe is astronomical distance. Stars and galaxies are observed whose light has been travelling billions of years to reach us. It is seldom mentioned by the Creationists because at the present time they have not discovered a means of refuting it, except to say that it is merely an appearance. The distance measurements are reliable and clearly refute the idea that the universe is only 10,000 years old.

The first step in establishing the distance of the stars was triangulation, using the opposite ends of the Earth's orbit around the Sun as a baseline. Measurement of the movement of a star relative to more distant stars allowed establishment of isosceles (equal sided) triangles which gave direct proportional measurements of the distance to the star. This technique (parallax) was first used successfully in the 1830s and has been in continuous use ever since. By 1964 parallaxes had been computed for 6,000 stars within approximately 300 light years (the distance that light travels in a year at 186,000 miles per second), but millions of stars are farther away than that.

Beginning in the late 1800s, scales of color and brightness were established. With these scales as a correction and the fact that brightness varies inversely as the square of the distance, measurements of clusters of stars were made that extended (by 1932) the range to approximately 55,000 light years, well beyond the 10,000 year limit of the Creationists.[23]

By the early 1900s many of the stars that had been observed were Cepheid variables. A variable star is one whose light fluctuates in a regular measurable pattern. The different classes of variables are named after the first star discovered, in this case delta Cepheus. The next step was the discovery in 1912 by Henrietta Leavitt that Cepheid variables have a fixed relationship between intrinsic (absolute) brightness and rate of pulsation. With measurement of any rate of pulsation, the intrinsic brightness of the variable is known. The comparison of the apparent brightness with the intrinsic brightness then gives a measurement of how far away the variable is. Since variables can be measured by other means in some of the nearer galaxies, the result was a scale for measuring the distance of more distant variables. These results are given in terms of hundreds of thousands of light years, far beyond the time span proposed by the Creationists. The observations and theories have been firm for decades, and consequently the scientific community has no doubt of their validity and no doubt of the impossibility of the Creationists' short time scale for the age of the universe.

The well-established reliability of this astronomical argument supports the geological and radiometric evidence for the great age of the Earth. The Creationist position forces denial of additional known astronomical explanations such as the ideas that impact cratering has a reliable correlation to age in the formation of planetary surfaces, that isotope ratios in planetary atmospheres correlate to age, or that excess heat radiated by Jupiter and Saturn is meaningful in establishing the origin of the planetary system. Creationists must also deny that energy radiating from the Sun's surface derives from the nuclear reactions of the core, since it takes millions of years for that energy to reach the surface.[24] Creationism also implies that, while the theory of stellar evolution is interesting and serves to connect a great variety of information that cannot otherwise be explained, it is basically irrelevant since there have not been billions of years during which the evolution took place.

To argue that this evidence is wrong or irrelevant because God created the Earth with only these appearances implies that God deliberately deceives our senses. His revelation through the natural world cannot be trusted and the combined effort of hundreds of thousands of scientists has been wasted. More clearly, all this supposed deception and waste is the consequence of accepting a faulty interpretation of Genesis and then seeking to fit all of the evidence to that interpretation. Creationists propose that the light from distant stars (at least those more than ten thousand light years away) was created "en route," and there is no way of knowing if the objects really exist. If one accepts this position, there is no assurance that the universe was not created yesterday with our memories intact. Such a conclusion seems incomprehensible. This odd position actually seems more related to skepticism and agnosticism than to the Scottish Common Sense Realism that most forebears of the Creationists believed. The conclusion of Creationism regarding astronomy is that order is an illusion, and causal relationships are a fantasy of the scientific mind.

Problems in Physics

Creationists must dispute something in each of the sciences. Even a field that seems remote, like physics, comes into the picture with the Creationists. For over twenty years the Creationists, especially Henry Morris and Duane Gish, have contended that the

Second Law of Thermodynamics contradicts evolution. The second law primarily summarizes the fact that in a closed system, energy tends to pass from an available form into a less available form. The Creationists believe that with ever-lessening amounts of useful energy, the evolutionary process with its growing complexity is a violation of the increasing entropy of the system. Scientists grant that this law applies to the universe as a whole, and to any closed system within it. They simply point out in response to the Creationist argument that the Earth and the biological subsystems upon it are not closed systems since there is a constant influx of energy from the Sun. The second law simply does not apply to evolution. In exactly the same manner that the Creationists use the law, it could also be used to demonstrate that the embryo cannot become an intricate adult because adults exhibit less entropy.

Mathematical Probability

A very disturbing issue is the misapplication of science in Creationist arguments. Disturbing because, if done out of ignorance, it calls into question their ability to engage in meaningful scientific discussion. If done knowingly, it calls their motives into question. This issue becomes clear in their use of mathematics.

One of the favorite Creationist lecture and debate techniques is to cite the extreme improbability of the evolution of some complex biological organism. There are several difficulties with the probability argument as posed by the Creationists. The most obvious is that it is basically irrelevant to discuss the probability of an event after it has happened. If the probability of rolling a two with a pair of dice is one in 36 and I do it on the thirteenth roll, the probability of doing is suddenly one, not one in 36 or even one in 13. Thus, it is basically inappropriate to apply probability to previous events.

A second difficulty is that Creationists often assume independence of events, which allows them to multiply probabilities instead of adding them, and thus getting exceedingly unlikely results. In essence they are placing events end to end when they should be side by side. Evolutionists consistently challenge the assumptions of the Creationists regarding the independence of events when calculating probabilities.

A third problem stems from the difficulties inherent in posing hypothetical probabilities. The probability that you of all the people in the world with access to books, of all the books currently in print, should be reading this one at this particular hour of all the hours since it hit the book stores is vanishingly small if independence is assumed, but you *are* reading this book.

Patterns

It would be possible to go on with specific arguments from Creationist sources and almost indefinitely discuss refutations from biological, geological and astronomical sources, for the literature has become vast in the last decade, but patterns of Creationist behavior are emerging. We first see that Creationists are not scientific in their methodology. They begin with presuppositions not subject to correction, not based in scientific evidence, but based upon their literal interpretation of the Bible. They err in attempting to create science from this interpretation, for they must operate from exceptions that fit their interpretation of the Bible, and must ignore evidence not consistent with their position. They ignore or deny the relevance of evidence rather than modify their position.

Creationists err in believing that a scientific theory depends for its validity upon its social or religious implications. Even if Creationists could somehow prove that belief in evolution leads to social decay, that would not logically demand that evolution is a false scientific theory. Science is not invalidated because it fails to lead to personal integration of the world view the Creationist desires.

In addition to methodological problems, Creationists do not practice science. They do little original research under laboratory conditions or in the field related to their biological and geological claims. There are several reasons for this. Most of them are not biologists or geologists, but as noted they are engineers, computer scientists, medical personnel and teachers at smaller, non-research-oriented colleges. Their institutions are publishing houses and speakers' bureaus with an occasional small museum, but they seldom have laboratories. When they have conducted research where it could be observed by the scientific community, it has frequently proven amateurish and even damaging to artifacts.[25] Those Creationists who do engage in research usually do it in unrelated areas or for industrial purposes which correlate poorly with their writings in biology and geology.

Most Creationist research consists of searching scientific literature for quotations that support their positions. This type of "proof-texting" frequently leads to selective quotation to the point of purporting to show that evolutionists themselves do not believe in evolution, or that evolutionists themselves admit that there is no evidence for evolution.[26] Scientific periodical literature is filled with evolutionist rebuttals and requests that the full context of their remarks be noted.[27] Creationists know the power of abbreviated quotes, for some only give permission for quotation from their works if the entire paragraph is cited. Related to the distortion of quotations is the indiscriminate use of sources. Evolutionists, Creationists and even ministers are all quoted on biological issues without identification, as if their understanding and opinions all had equal scientific validity and carried equal weight.

Additional evidence that Creationists are not practicing science includes their spirit of completeness and finality (dogmatism) in their work, which is antithetical to the openness inherent in the scientific method. Dogmatism combined with a lack of research means they do not publish in the scientific literature. In the past, they claimed there was a conspiracy to prevent publication of Creationist papers in the scientific journals, which forced them to publish privately. The benefit was that the private publication proved profitable, and scientific publication usually is not. We should note that the scientific journals do publish letters from Creationists on a regular basis.

Still another evidence of the non-scientific nature of Creationism is that they do not appeal to the knowledgeable scientific community for evaluation of their work. Rather, they appeal to the public, which has little knowledge of appropriate criteria for evaluation. This betrays a basic distrust of the self-correcting mechanism within the scientific method because it sometimes works very slowly. Since the Creationists have been successful in swaying public opinion, the scientific evaluation of their work has followed, and it has been devastating.

Testing Creationism

Creationism is not science because it seldom presents a comprehensive theory that is testable. The "science" Creationists present is a negative and inaccurate refutation of evolution that is supposed to prove Creationism in a restricted one-alternative system. Even the frequently occurring comparative tables of the "two models" (evolution and creation) are only fragmentary statements of theories. While they have been relatively successful in establishing the two-model approach and eliminating other alternatives, one consequence is that they have been placed on the defensive as evidence against their position has accumulated.[28]

At the few points where their model presents testable hypotheses, especially the 10,000 year age of the universe, the evidence is conclusively against them. Independent biological, geological, radiometric and astronomical evidence overwhelmingly points to the great age of the cosmos. They have consistently sought to collapse the geological record into a single event, the biblical Flood. They have struggled to explain the formation of fossils in the few months the Flood allows. They have sought to find evidence of accelerated deposition of rock during a worldwide flood. They have tried to explain the fossil sequence by theories of survival of more agile animals at higher elevation. They have not provided convincing evidence. The result has not been a unified theory that leads to new research or makes verifiable predictions. The result has been a series of *ad hoc* explanations to patch the holes created by scientific criticism.

One testable prediction they have made is that Man and the dinosaurs were contemporaneous. This prediction has resulted in the Creationist equivalent of the Piltdown hoax that they traditionally cite against the evolutionist. In the 1930s a paleontologist, Roland A. Bird, saw a piece of limestone in a store window with what were supposed to be fossilized human footprints. The supposed location of this find was the Paluxy riverbed near Glen Rose, Texas. Travelling to the site and excavating there Bird found many dinosaur prints, which he shipped to museums, but no human ones. Apparently, the citizens had carved some of the human prints, and others were formed from partially obliterated three-toed dinosaur tracks.

In 1950 Clifford L. Burdick printed an article in the Seventh Day Adventist journal, *The Signs of the Times*, from which Henry Morris borrowed the story for *The Genesis Flood* (1960), spreading this "evidence" for Creationism more widely. To the credit of the Adventists, they eventually realized the dubious nature of the prints and printed a debunking article in 1975 by Berney Neufeld in *Origins*, complete with photographs showing three-toed dinosaur prints, and not human prints. Neufeld also obtained photos of museum specimens that showed compaction under the dinosaur tracks and none under the human prints, implying that the latter had been carved.[29]

Other Creationists were unconvinced by Neufeld, however, and in 1982 Carl Baugh began new excavations on the Paluxy River. Baugh invited skeptical scientists to join him, and they did. Laurie Godfrey of the University of Massachusetts at Amherst, Steven Schaferman of Northern Iowa University, and Ronnie Hastings evaluated the best findings of Baugh's team. The "footprints" were up to sixteen inches long, which the Creationists attributed to the giantism mentioned in Genesis 6:4. Most of the prints had the "big toe" in the middle, unlike any human or ape footprints. Most others had no discernible features that would identify them as footprints. The stride length was inconsistent, varying with each step, and the direction changed with each step. The "footprints" further changed size and shape with each step. By contrast, the dinosaur trails were sharp, clear, consistent and easy to spot.[30] The scientists concluded that the "footprints" were the result of typical leaching and erosion in most cases, and since others were in line and properly spaced with dinosaur tracks, they concluded that they were the middle toe impressions of a three-toed dinosaur.[31] In 1985 an entire issue of *Creation/Evolution*, a journal opposed to Creationism, was devoted to the Paluxy River footprints. These articles offered several explanations for the human characteristics of some tracks, and demonstrated that others were imperfect dinosaur tracks. Following extensive research, sympathetic Christian Glen J. Kuban reached essentially the same conclusion. The ICR and others have stopped using the Paluxy River prints as evidence against evolution.[32]

The example of contemporaneous human and dinosaur footprints represents an attempt to disprove evolution by transferring a mathematical method of proof to the physical world, namely, proof by counterexample. Even were the prints authentic, the case for coexistence would be based on an anomaly, whereas there are hundreds of sites where no human prints have been found with dinosaur prints, or human bones with dinosaur bones. While exceptions sometimes lead to new theories, the normal situation is that science is built on the rule, not the exception.

The debate platform has also proved a testing ground for Creationism. The Creationists initially roundly defeated the scientists in campus debates because the scientists took them too lightly and were unprepared for their arguments. In recent years that trend has reversed, several instances of embarrassing mistakes by Creationists have accumulated, and the number of debates has fallen off. A more common occurrence now is for videos of older debates to be shown in Creationist meetings.

A consequence of these trends in the Creationist method, especially the lack of peer review, is that Creationist errors and fallacies persist long after they have been demonstrated to be false.[33] A very compact collection of disproven "myths" of Creationism may be found on a videocassette from Swaggert Ministries entitled "That I May Know Him." On this cassette Jimmy Swaggert repeats the tale of Joshua's Missing Day and the NASA scientists who discovered it on their computers, an impossible tale because of the inadequacy of ancient astronomical records. The story was borrowed from Harold Hill, who has been unable to provide proof of the legitimacy of the story. A second fallacy that Swaggert repeats is that morality is inheritable, based upon the famous Jukes family and the descendants of Jonathan Edwards. A third myth is the "Lady Hope" story of the woman who allegedly heard Darwin's deathbed conversion. For an overly-critical but sound refutation of these stories, see Tom McIver, "Ancient Tales and Space Age Myths of Creationist Evangelism," *The Skeptical Inquirer* 10 (Spring, 1986).

Still another persistent myth is Duane Gish's use of the Bombardier Beetle, which supposedly mixes two explosive chemicals in its attempts to make itself unattractive to predators. Gish's argument is that the beetle could not have evolved because it would have exploded before the inhibitor could have evolved. In actuality the two chemicals, hydrogen peroxide and hydroquinone, are not explosive, but the myth persists in both Gish's books and those who quote him, even though this was publically exposed in debate as early as 1978. Scientific refutations can frequently be ignored by the Creationists because they occur in journals unlikely to be read by their followers.

What Creationists must be credited with is marvelous political skill and immense success in getting science debated in the public arena. They have largely succeeded in convincing the American people that their perspective should be taught in the public schools. In the long run, it is at least possible that serious consequences for freedom of religion could follow as local school boards and educators discover what the scientific community already knows.

Another question remains. Even though it appears that Creationism is not scientific, could it still be true, on the basis of the Bible? Perhaps the framework of science is totally false and inconsistent with the Bible, even though it agrees with the observed world, that is, the natural revelation. These questions make it necessary to address in the following chapter the issue of whether the proper interpretation of the Bible forces us to a Creationist position.

The Creationist Interpretation of the Bible

Many Creationists are sincere warm-hearted Christians. They frequently are compassionate, concerned about the well-being of others, effective church members, worthy citizens, and loving parents. They are unstintingly orthodox with regard to the divinity of Christ, and fidelity to their understanding of the Word of God is unquestioned. Nevertheless, they are often rigid and closed to Christians with alternate perceptions of what the Word of God says. Sincerity cannot be equated with infallible judgment, appropriate scientific knowledge, or acceptable exegesis of the Scriptures. This chapter sets out the evidence that Creationists, with regard to origins, have selected an inappropriate point of view that is unfaithful to the Scriptures.

One of the primary concerns of both Christian conservatives and Fundamentalists is the loss of the transcendent in American society; that is, the sense of the presence of God and the sense of wonder when surveying the universe. Much of this loss conservatives place at the feet of the system of higher education. In 1976 Edward Norman wrote, "There is no doubt that in developed societies education has contributed to the decline of religious belief."[1] A survey of higher education indicates that the one conception that seems most pervasive across disciplinary lines is the developmental hypothesis; that is, a generalized evolution. By blurring the distinction between evolution as social progress and evolution in organic processes, conservatives and Fundamentalists alike have accepted the perception that more cases of loss of faith are due to evolution than anything else. Much of Creationist theory is thus rooted in concern over the social implications of belief in evolutionary theory.

Unfortunately, Creationism is based upon an inappropriate, incomplete and at times even false hermeneutic. Hermeneutics is the logical ordering and identification of appropriate principles in the process of interpreting a document or biblical passage. The principles of hermeneutics have been frequently analyzed and largely agreed upon by biblical and literary scholars.[2] In the process of interpretation three steps are necessary: determining the normative or basic (not necessarily literal) meaning of a passage, determining the author's reason or purpose for a passage, and establishing the implications of the passage. These must be held in balance, and none can safely be neglected.

The process of interpretation also involves both subjective and objective determinants on the part of the interpreter. The subjective determinants for a given passage are its common sense, its spiritual sense, and its experiential sense, or a meaning made relevant based upon the individual experience of the interpreter. The subjective elements are what have given Christian preaching and writing its excitement and variety over the centuries. The subjective elements are essential. Again, erroneous interpretation may result from the overemphasis on one of these senses to the neglect of the others.

Objective determinants include such elements as etymology (the origin and development of words), synonyms, comparative philology (mastering the comparative meaning of words across language and social barriers), historical context, social context, author's purpose and viewpoint and other similar elements. Mis-interpretation of biblical passages is usually the result of neglect of the objective determinants of a biblical passage. A consequence of the Creationist neglect of these elements is the loss of the wealth of accumulated studies in Christian tradition over the past 2000 years.

The primary focus of Creationist biblical interpretation is literalism, taking the "face value" of a passage, usually meaning its apparent immediate meaning to me at the present time, while neglecting its historical meaning. Creationists believe that the Scriptures, especially Genesis chapters one and two, should be interpreted literally. However, it is of course impossible for anyone to be a thorough-going literalist—the Lord is not literally my shepherd, for I am not a sheep. The problem for the literalist is that he wrongly equates the literal with the historical and the true, while he equates the symbolic with the non-historical and false. In reality, the literalist spirit betrays the bondage of the technologically-oriented person to modern culture, not to the Bible, since the dominance of science and technology in our society leads to the neglect of the literary approach to interpretation which involves thinking symbolically. As Conrad Hyers has said, "Poetry is turned into prose, truth into statistics, understanding into facts, education into note taking, art into criticism, symbols into signs, faith into beliefs."[3] To take "the Lord is my shepherd" literally is obviously false, while the true meaning of the phrase from the 23rd Psalm involves understanding that the intent of the passage is to indicate that the Lord is the guide and protector. Since the crucial issue is whether it is appropriate to interpret Genesis One literally, we must evaluate the consequences of ignoring the subjective and objective elements in interpreting that passage.

The first step in the literalism of the Creationists is a tendency to fragment Genesis One; that is, to remove it from its context and break it into pieces. Genesis One is not an isolated collection of verses, detached from the Mosaic history and law that was directed toward helping a monotheistic tribal people become a nation. The core meaning, as will be seen in detail later, is the rejection of polytheism, not the origin of the universe, the Earth or even of life. Genesis One is a Hebrew apologetic catechism which seeks to demonstrate that no created being or physical feature of the Earth or heavens is worthy of worship. All such things and the Earth itself were creations of the one true God.

Decontextualization and fragmentation are compounded by dogmatism. Claims to knowing the one true interpretation of any passage are simply not tenable. Consideration of any passage shows clearly that many meanings have been observed over the centuries, and these have changed with the social context to some extent. But a sound hermeneutical method does place bounds on how far the exegetical process can be carried.

Yet another interpretive error into which Creationists may fall is to assume that the Bible presents a systematized view. For the most part, the writings in the Bible arose in response to particular moral problems common to Man, not physical or environmental problems. The general applicability of a passage of Scripture to the estate of Man is sometimes destroyed by universalizing a particular detail that was relevant only at a particular time and place. Universalizing is a chronic danger for theologians trying to create systematic theology from the Bible, a situation even more aggravated when the Creationists attempt to create a systematic science from the Bible. This does not mean that biblical statements should be ignored, but it does mean that they do not present a complete picture of the natural world. The Bible presents common-sense explanations of everyday phenomena in a fashion comprehensible to its hearers and readers, but not to twentieth-century scientific explanations. By not being scientific, it is not erroneous, fallacious or uninspired. The science was appropriate for the purpose.

Related to the error of finding a complete system is the encyclopedic error in interpreting the Bible. This is not just an assumption that the Bible presents a system of science; it goes beyond that to assume that the Bible presents all that is necessary for one to know about a topic. To appeal to the Bible as the final scientific authority implies that it can answer the necessary and essential scientific questions. While the Evangelical Christian expects to find spiritual guidance and the solution to sin in the Bible, expecting to find a solution to sociological, historical, psychological, and scientific questions is expecting what the Bible does not deliver. God has given us the ability to search for these answers. It was not necessary that He reveal them to us.

The interpretive issues outlined above are the ones of primary concern with regard to Creationist exegesis of the Genesis passage (and other passages including Isaiah 40). The first essential of interpretation is the placing of a passage in context. Context means paying attention to the structure and idiom of the language. For example, Genesis One exhibits in Hebrew a significant amount of rhyming, a recurrent rhythm, and a great deal of repetition, especially of certain phrases like "The evening and the morning were...." These three elements are common to Hebrew poetry, and commentaries upon the passage across the centuries have noted that. There are, however, significant departures from pure Hebrew poetic form. Symbolism is less prominent than in poetic passages from the Psalms, and the sense of real objects is so prominent as to suggest that some of the elements of prose are also present in the passage. The best conclusion is that this is a mixed type of literature combining poetry and prose. The combination eliminates some of the options for this passage. Due to its semi-poetic nature, it is unlikely to be a pure history, but neither is it one of the other types of biblical literature such as typology, allegory, symbolism or apocalypticism.

The complexity of its literary context forces a serious look at its historical context. The first two chapters of Genesis provide an introduction to the history of God's interaction with and the spiritual biography of a nomadic tribe that migrated to Egypt, became captive, escaped, and due to its size had to have a system of governance. Most of the Pentateuch is their history and law. The most persistent problem throughout Israel's history is not evil leaders, war with neighbors, poor tools, or any such problem. The basic issue was the chronic temptation to fall into the worship of the gods of the surrounding peoples. The very introduction to their history is then a statement of why the Israelites will not follow other gods, namely that these gods are the work of men who are the creation of the one true God. This statement of the necessity of monotheism was put into an easily remembered form so that it could be readily learned and transmitted from generation to generation. This historical context makes suspect the idea that this catechism is a definitive scientific statement of origins.

The consideration of the historical context leads to the second most essential principle of hermeneutics, namely that no part of the Bible should be interpreted apart from the whole. Several parts of that whole are essential to a proper interpretation of Genesis One. While the biblical revelation is historical, as has been increasingly demonstrated by archaeological discovery over the past century, it is also progressive. God is not fully revealed in the Pentateuch. Probably the most essential characteristic of God other than his taking sin seriously is the sense of absolute truth and truthfulness that he represents.[4] When the Creationists suggest even in passing that God could create a deception—that is, that he could create a "mature" universe with the appearance of age, or that he created artifacts that would imply age to the observer—they violate this principle of hermeneutics. God's creation is an accurate representation of the past. We must seek to interpret both the past and the Bible appropriately.

The basic method of interpretation over the centuries has been the historico-grammatical method. This method requires interpretation to fit the facts of grammar and the facts of history (including science). During both the Patristic period and the Middle Ages, the use of allegorical and symbolical interpretive methodologies on the part of Catholic scholars led to some excesses. A tradition of superinterpretation developed, that is, attributing to a passage much more significance than is actually implicit in it. When the Protestant Reformation occurred, the reaction to the interpretive methods of Catholic scholars pushed the Protestants toward a literalistic interpretive methodology which has persisted for over four hundred years. That tradition of literalism has now been so well developed that we are experiencing superinterpretation far beyond the implications of Genesis One at the opposite extreme from the past.

Finally, exegesis of any passage must be theologically informed. This requirement is not unrelated to what has already been said about the nature of God. What it means is, where does this passage fit in the theological pattern of the Bible? Fitting a passage theologically comes with maturity and long practice in much the same way that some of the most insightful histories have come from older scholars. The problem for the Creationists is that they are not interrelated well with the rest of the Church. They do not interact with the best theology of the past or present, and they are influenced little by the interpretive traditions of the past.

Despite a long and readily available history of the proper use of hermeneutics, some Creationists seem unaware of these principles, or they imply that they are a complication introduced to make it difficult for the individual to interpret the Bible for himself. Their misconception concerning proper exegesis appears in the occasional statements that they are not interpreting the Scriptures at all, but are just taking the plain meaning. They imply that those who observe the complexities of proper interpretation are distorting the meaning. The "plain" meaning is a form of exegesis and in some cases may be an incomplete or inadequate meaning.

A second inadequacy of their exegesis is that they are only selectively literal. While they wish for the days of Genesis One to be literal twenty-four-hour periods, they would not wish for the Great Day of the Lord in the New Testament to be limited to a single twenty-four-hour day. They do not insist that the Sun circles the Earth, as Joshua 10:12-13 would imply if interpreted literally. Creationists are not in the streets calling for the killing of all women who commit adultery, although that is a part of the Mosaic law. Neither do they recommend cutting off the hands of all thieves. They have rejected the "clear and unmistakable flat-earth teaching of the Bible" that John Hampden upheld just a century ago, which caused him to affirm that it was impossible to believe modern astronomy and accept the Scriptures.[5] The compromises of the Fundamentalists with the literal meaning of the Bible are endless, which makes the adherence to a twenty-four hour day in Genesis One all the more unfortunate.

The Creationists want only one meaning in a passage, the historical—no double meanings, no complex layers, no beautiful matrices of interwoven thought. All this is collapsed into the "simple." This seems a most awkward allowing of culture to shape the interpretive methodology. The twentieth-century Western technological one-right-answer mentality leads Creationists to abandon the richness of the biblical fabric for a straight string. Their understanding of meaning in literature seems so limited that they cannot perceive the representational and symbolic as anything other than the opposite of literal and therefore false. The preoccupation of our society with efficiency leads to the "one right answer" also being regarded as the best answer because it saves time or simplifies. This mind-set is at odds with the Hebrew tradition in which the Old Testament was cast. This tradition was pastoral, with time not an issue. The flow of thought was directed toward contemplation, a consideration of issues from more than one perspective with many parallelisms. Much of this cultural richness is lost in Creationist writing and interpretation.

The consequence of this inappropriate hermeneutic is that the Bible is pitted against science, and the natural revelation appears at odds with the special revelation. Science, in part, developed as an outgrowth of the Christian commitment to explore all of God's creation. This harmonic view of nature and theology and the appropriateness of pursuing science as a "call" from God have been lost subsequent to the Enlightenment as those antagonistic to the faith sought to purify science from the influence of religion. Following the successful secularization of science during the nineteenth century, we have reached the point today where the National Academy of Sciences could issue a resolution in 1981 stating, "Religion and Science are separate and mutually exclusive realms of human thought whose presentation in the same context leads to misunderstanding of both scientific theory and religious belief."[6] This statement implies that modern science is dependent upon a philosophical/theological propositions that the universe and the processes of its creation are independent of God and that he is not interactive with it at present. The statement also seems to ignore that science as a philosophy of positivism is different from science as a practice of the discovery of the order and the operation of the universe. Tragically, the Creationists have accepted both the dichotomy and the antagonism and have come to view science as the ugly offspring of the Enlightenment.

The Enlightenment becomes in the Creationist perspective an unfortunate occurrence in human history. Some Creationists grant that the Enlightenment provided freedom from restrictions to explore God's creation more fully. However, because some used that freedom to attack Christianity (especially attacking the Roman Catholic Church), the roots of the Enlightenment in Christian toleration are no longer considered by the Creationists, and the Enlightenment has become allied in their thinking with pagan intolerance of Christianity. This is the picture of the past that the Creationist sees, yet the Creationist himself enjoys the freedom to challenge established science as a consequence of the religious toleration built into our Constitution. Toleration in the United States was a result of the ideals of Christian charity and Enlightenment toleration that infused the Constitutional Convention.

While the sociological concern over an unnecessary war against science is serious, an even more critical concern for the Christian is the evidence that Creationists are distorting the very core of Christian faith. The movement enlists followers to a cause that does not keep Christ's atonement for Man's sin as the central focus of Christianity. By placing the view of the process of creation at the heart of what separates Christian from pagan, a serious deformity is introduced. Creationists have been unable to decide whether to focus on evolution as a religion, or whether to detach "scientific creationism" from Christianity. They have tried both, leading to confusion. While evolution has philosophical underpinnings which have theological consequences, that does not make it a religion, except in the hands of enthusiasts like Carl Sagan. On the other hand, attempts to detach Creationism from the Bible seem an unfortunate subordination of science to the court system. Such attempts occurred in the Arkansas and Louisiana court cases which sought to avoid the issue of involvement of the state in promoting religion. This is a much less admirable movement than the original straightforward evangelism of Henry Morris and others when the movement was revived three decades ago. [7]

As noted previously, Creationism has also moved the defense of the Christian faith from more historically established areas such as the historicity of Christ and the reasons for the sudden growth of Christianity in the first three centuries to the much more speculative area of origins. The issue becomes much less accessible to the layperson because of the complexity of the science involved. Further, readers become much more vulnerable to false arguments because they cannot understand the content of the arguments. The essence of the Creationist movement is that it has replaced the core of Christianity with a peripheral issue.

Finally, the Creationists have dangerously replaced the moral core of Christianity with an intellectual issue. The evidence of this is the acceptance into the movement of those who have a case against evolution regardless of their position concerning the person of Christ. When a Hindu astronomer is called to testify on behalf of Creationists, as was the case in Arkansas, it has to be considered a subversion of the professed desire of Creationists to bring society back to a Christian foundation. While it is true that Christians have allied themselves in the past with non-Christians on behalf of great social causes, there is a subtle difference in the present situation. The earlier movements allied with unbelievers to effect social change, the need for which was rooted in their Christian perceptions. The Creationists ally themselves with unbelievers in a social cause against evolution, believing that it will establish the validity of the Bible in the eyes of the faithless, a proposition unlikely to succeed.

The almost inevitable downfall of a movement based upon poor science and an inadequate hermeneutic will cause embarrassment to the Christian faith, especially since the Creationists claim as Henry Morris does that one cannot obtain a true understanding of anything without accepting Genesis as literally true in its scientific inferences.[8] The polemical efforts of all Christians will be damaged by the use of false means to achieve the worthy end of defending the faith. Misinterpreting the Bible in a fashion that leads to false conclusions about science is not a viable system of thought. It is not an acceptable alternative to atheistic naturalism. The following chapter contains a consideration of the political consequences of poor science and distorted theology.

The Political/ Legal Strategy of the Creationists

During the last three decades Creationism has evolved into a political movement which some Fundamentalists are using to gain power. Through massive literature distribution in the churches and through direct mail, large numbers of Christians have been convinced of the validity of the Creationist position, and their influence has become pervasive in the Christian private school movement.

Once the Creationists had established a large power base within the church, especially among the Baptist conventions and the independent churches, the next target was the public schools. Since the presentation of evolution cannot be completely eliminated, Creationists have moved to introduce Creationism into the curriculum on the basis of fairness or balanced treatment. They have sought textbook changes, some of which are legitimate, especially where our religious heritage has been completely ignored. On the local level, Creationists have pressed to have evolutionary teaching suppressed, a violation of free academic inquiry for both teachers and students.

This educational thrust has involved the Creationists in sustained legal conflict related to a variety of church-state issues. In chapter three we considered the initial stages of the legal involvement, a few of which continue into the present. As noted previously, five states eventually passed anti-evolution statutes. With the demise of the statewide anti-evolution legal crusade, the Fundamentalists seeking changes in curriculum and textbook content turned to state and local boards of education. Several states limited or suppressed the use of texts which espoused evolution.

The return of evolution to the forefront of educational and legal controversy was precipitated by Sputnik in 1957. The renewed conflict had three aspects. Creationists attacked the scientific validity of evolution, pursued legal redress for abridgement of Constitutional rights and pressured school boards and textbook publishers to omit evolution and/or include Creationism. The three aspects are intertwined and can only be separated artificially, but discussing them seperately is useful in unraveling the complexity of the issues. The current consideration, then, is what has been occurring in the court system as the Creationists have sought legislation, filed suits, and themselves been sued.

The Constitutional Issues

There are two clauses in the First Amendment to the United States Constitution. The first clause prohibits Congress from making any laws that would establish religion; the second clause prevents Congress from passing laws prohibiting the free exercise of religion. The Supreme Court has significantly adjusted the interpretation of these two clauses since World War II.[1]

The establishment clause had been of little significance since the early nineteenth century when the last established state church disappeared in the United States. However, in 1947 the Supreme Court through the opinion of Justice Hugo Black in *Everson v. Board of Education* applied the metaphor of a "wall of separation" between the Church and the state beyond the national level. The Court extended the metaphor to the state and local governments, although it upheld the New Jersey reimbursement of bus fare to private and parochial school students' parents.[2] The following year, in 1948, separation was the basis for striking down the provision of classroom religious instruction by ministers of local churches in *McCullom v. Board of Education*.

It was not until 1962, however, that the Fundamentalists were thoroughly aroused. In that year the Court in *Engel v. Vitale* forbade state-sponsored prayer in the schools.[3] Even non-denominational and non-compulsory prayer was ruled inconsistent with the establishment clause. This ruling affected laws in eighteen states that provided for prayer in the schools.[4] In 1963 in *Abington School District v. Schempp*, the mandatory reading of Bible verses and recitation of the Lord's Prayer were struck down.

In the *Schempp* opinion, however, as the Court sought to avert the charge of hostility toward religion, Justice Tom C. Clark's opinion noted that a religion of secularism could not be favored by overt hostility toward traditional religion.[5] The Fundamentalists have attempted to use this decision to secure a legal foundation for a variety of positions. One of the early claims was that the Biological Sciences Curriculum Study (BSCS) textbooks with obvious evolutionary teaching represented just such antagonism and the establishment of a religion of secularism.

Equal Time for Creationism

In 1963, in the face of the BSCS capture of half the textbook market, Nell Segraves argued that neutrality under *Schempp* required the teaching of Creationism alongside evolution. Failure to do this, and teaching evolution alone, was a violation of freedom to believe, just as reciting Bible verses was a violation of freedom to disbelieve under *Schempp*. In 1963 Segraves and Jean Sumrall petitioned the California Board of Education for relief. While they did not initially succeed, they did secure a ruling from Max Rafferty, the Superintendent of Public Instruction, that evolution be identified as a theory.

The concept of equal time was slow to develop, but in 1964 and 1965 bills were introduced in Arizona in support of equal time for Creationism. Both of these bills died in committee. During the last half of the 1960s the concept of equal time as an alternative to excluding evolution spread widely.

On the other side, the National Education Association (NEA) was seeking a means of using *Schempp* to strike down the remaining anti-evolution laws. On behalf of the Arkansas Education

Association, Susan Epperson filed for a declaratory judgment against the Arkansas law as a violation of freedom of speech. The trial judge was openly hostile toward the statute and scheduled the trial for April Fool's Day, allowed the case only a one day hearing, and refused to admit expert testimony. When the Arkansas Attorney General sought to introduce evidence against evolution, he was prevented by the judge, who reasoned, as in Scopes, that the issue was a state's authority over employees versus the employee's constitutional rights. Judge Reed ruled against the statute on unarticulated constitutional grounds, but did not rule on whether evolution could be taught as fact or whether Creationism could be taught alongside evolution, which were not issues in the case but were matters of strong public interest.[7]

In 1967 a suit was filed against Tennessee's anti-evolution statute. The case was deferred when legislation to repeal was introduced. The repealer easily passed the House, but in the Senate the bill surprisingly failed on a 16 to 16 vote. Meanwhile, a temporary teacher, Gary L. Scott, was fired in rural Campbell County for describing the Bible as a collection of fairy tales. William M. Kunstler, the ACLU and the National Science Teachers Association (NSTA) all came to Scott's aid. The Campbell County School Board reinstated Scott with back pay. Under pressure, the Tennessee Senate then revoted, and the anti-evolution law was repealed.

On June 5, 1967, events took an unusual turn when the Arkansas Supreme Court reversed *Epperson* in a two-sentence opinion stating that the law was within the state's right to control curriculum in the public schools.[8] Susan Epperson immediately appealed to the Supreme Court. There Epperson's attorney argued that evolution was established science. He was supported by briefs from the National Science Teachers Association (NSTA) and the NEA. He also claimed that the law was an abridgement of academic freedom. The State of Arkansas, under a new Attorney General, disassociated itself from the law and defended only the right of the state to set the curriculum in the schools, whether educational groups approved of the curriculum or not. The Court ruled against the Arkansas Act on the basis that restricting evolutionary teaching had a religious purpose of promoting Protestant Fundamentalism in violation of the establishment clause. Edward

Larson, who made the most thorough study of these cases, concludes that changing public opinion had more to do with striking the law than did legal precedent.[9] Nevertheless, *Epperson* left the Mississippi anti-evolution law as the only one still in the statute books.

Mrs. Arthur G. Smith filed suit against the Mississippi law in 1969. Since Mississippi had no declaratory judgment procedure, the alternative was to seek an injunction against enforcement. The state moved to dismiss the action since the law only precluded teaching Darwinism as fact and since the absence of any enforcement made the injunction unnecessary. Early in 1970 a repealer was filed in the state legislature. After floor debate reminiscent of forty years earlier, the repeal failed 42 to 70. The atmosphere in Mississippi was more resistant because of desegregation pressures at the same time. The pre-trial motion to dismiss was granted, and on appeal the case rose to the Mississippi Supreme Court. The Mississippi Supreme Court ruled against the law on the basis of *Epperson*, but pointedly indicated that Biblical Creationism could be taught in the schools as well. On the basis of its success, this would be the course of action that the Creationists hereafter would pursue.

In 1969 the California State Board of Education approved the *Science Framework*, which identified creation and evolution as historical scientific theories which were validly taught in the public schools. Nell Segraves and her son Kelly joined with Henry Morris to form the Creation-Science Research Center to generate teaching materials for the public schools. The older Creation Research Society also produced a book called *Biology: A Search for Order in Complexity*.

In Texas Mel and Norma Gabler led a movement to remove the BSCS texts from the approved list of books. These efforts in California and Texas marked the 1970s as a decade in which the Creationists' goals were to reduce the theory of evolution to a hypothesis and to introduce Creationism as an hypothesis of equal validity.

The leaders remained essentially the same in the 1970s. Henry Morris and the ICR provided "scientific support" of Creationist educational and legal efforts. Nell and Kelly Segraves used the Creation-Science Research Center to support legal efforts to teach

Creationism. Paul Ellwanger founded Citizens for Fairness in Education, which distributed draft legislation for use at local and state levels. On the other side the active opponents continued to be the ACLU, the NEA, the NSTA and a new addition, the American Jewish Congress. Scientific organizations issuing pronouncements against Creationism included the American Association for the Advancement of Science, the National Academy of Sciences and the National Association of Biology Teachers.

Creationist legal efforts were unsuccessful in the early 1970s. In Texas, Rita Wright's case was dismissed, a case in which it was asserted that teaching evolution as fact represented a direct attack on religion. Upon appeal a federal appellate court affirmed the dismissal, and the United States Supreme Court refused to hear the case further. William T. Willoughby's 1972 case against the NSF for funding the BSCS series met a similar fate. Dale Crowley's case against evolutionary displays at the Smithsonian joined Willoughby's in being dismissed, the dismissal affirmed by the appellate court and the Supreme Court refusing to hear it. This action effectively eliminated challenging evolution as a limited scientific theory which was not legitimate for public display, and it forced Creationists toward greater emphasis upon efforts to secure equal time.

Renewed Equal Time Effort

The renewed equal time effort began in 1973 in Tennessee. The legislation submitted required that evolution be taught as a theory, not as a scientific fact. Texts presenting evolution were to give equal time to other theories of origins, including the Genesis account. The legislators responded in accord with public opinion about the fairness of equal time, and the bill passed within three weeks.[10]

The law was challenged almost immediately by the National Association of Biology Teachers and Americans United for the Separation of Church and State. The contention of these organizations was that the law represented the establishment of religion. The legal cases proceeded on state and federal levels concurrently, with the federal appellate court acting first. The court declared that the law was patently unconstitutional for mandating the teaching of the Bible in the public schools and for involving the state in attempting to identify Satanic theories, which the law required to be excluded. This defeat encouraged the Creationists, who believed the law only suffered technical flaws. They intended to learn from this mistake.

By this time the Creationists had called forth organized resistance to their efforts. Journals such as the *Skeptical Inquirer*, which normally debunks ESP, saucer cultists, table rappers and spoon benders, turned its attention to Creationism. *Physics Today* called upon physicists nationwide to secure copies of CRS tactical booklets in order to appear at local school board meetings to combat the Creationists. *Sky and Telescope* and *Astronomy* carried articles about the threat that Creationism posed in that science. Alarms sounded over pressure on the NSF to distribute funding to Creationists. The scientific community no longer ignored Creationism.

In California, 1972 was the year for adopting new biology texts under the 1970 *Science Framework*. A flood of protest from the scientific community arose over the inclusion of Creationism. The result of this protest was a compromise where Creationism was not included, but evolution was presented more conditionally than previously. By 1974 the Creationist provisions of the *Science Framework* had been dropped.[11] The modification of the *Science Framework* by the California Board of Education was supported by the state Attorney General, who reasoned that teaching biological evolution neither directly nor indirectly advanced atheism.

In the light of the situation in California, in 1974 the Texas Board of Education adopted a resolution requiring textbooks to treat evolution as one of several theories of origins that were not factually verifiable. The Texas Board then rejected all three versions of the BSCS series as not meeting the resolution. Since this ruling did not mandate teaching Creationism, it survived for over a decade without legal challenge. It is frequently credited with reducing the emphasis upon evolution nationwide by as much as 50 percent over the ten years it was in effect from 1974 to 1984.[12]

In December 1975 the Indiana Textbook Commission adopted the Creationist text, *Biology: A Search for Order in Complexity* as a seventh statewide approved text. The intent was that the book supplement one of the other six texts. Five local districts adopted it in that manner, but the West Clark Community Schools adopted only the Creationist text and thus potentially violated the Epperson decision. After a hearing by the textbook Commission at which it reaffirmed approval of the text, the members sought to divorce themselves from the actions of the West Clark Board. Upon legal appeal the Indianapolis trial court judge Michael T. Dugan agreed with the ACLU that the book was sectarian and unfit for public school use. The Indiana Textbook Commission dropped the text without further appeal.

Kentucky approached the problem somewhat differently in 1976 by passing legislation giving teachers the option of teaching creation from the Bible. The bill imposed no restrictions on either pupil or teacher, did not challenge evolution as science, and remains in effect to the present.

For a time legal activity, especially as it related to textbooks, was reduced until 1981. In California Kelly Segraves of the CSRC filed suit to prevent the teaching of evolution which was seen as establishment of the religion of secular humanism, and a burden upon the free exercise of religion by Christians. Segraves lost the case, but the judge instructed the California State Board of Education to reissue its anti-dogmatism regulations to all school districts.[13]

Elsewhere, the renewed legal impetus to Creationism was provided by Wendell Bird. Bird was a brilliant student who had converted from a self-described theistic evolutionary position to Creationism. After completing Yale Law School, he joined the ICR as a legal consultant. In mid-1979 a resolution written by Bird for adoption by local school boards and seeking to provide balance through equal time provisions was distributed extensively by the ICR. Paul Ellwanger, a physical therapist who founded Citizens for Fairness in Education in 1977, adapted Bird's resolution into model legislation that was proposed in South Carolina in 1979 (and failed), in eight states in 1980 and in fourteen states in 1981. In 1981 state senator James L. Holsted submitted the bill in Arkansas where it swept through the legislature in three weeks and was promptly signed by the governor two days later.[14]

The Arkansas Case

The Arkansas statute required treatment of both evolution and Creationism in all schools teaching either theory. Louisiana followed with legislation that same year after a bill that still treated Creationism as religion died in committee in 1980. The Louisiana Senate version allowed the teaching of Creationism as a local option, resembling more closely the Kentucky legislation. The House, however, added provisions requiring teaching of both positions and in all state-supported schools prohibited discrimination against Creationists who might apply for positions. This included the state colleges and universities.[15]

The ACLU brought suit against the more vulnerable Arkansas law first. The case came to trial late in 1981 with the ACLU attempting primarily to affirm that Creationism was not science at all, but was a Fundamentalist religious apologetic. The constitutional issue focused on the establishment clause requirement that the state have a secular purpose and that it have the effect of neither advancing nor inhibiting religion. The ACLU argued that the equal time law advanced religion. The court rejected Wendell Bird's petition to intervene as an additional party on behalf of the Creationists.[16] Bird accused Attorney General Steve Clark of inadequate preparation and an insincere support of the legislation. Clark in turn accused Bird of unwillingness to cooperate as a team member, of insistence on primary leadership which Clark felt was his responsibility as Attorney General, and of witness tampering. Clark was hampered in his ability to find witnesses who had not put in writing their religious motivation for promoting Creationism, as was the case with most prominent leaders like Morris and Gish. Clear statements of intent to convert by supporters undercut Clark's attempts to establish a secular purpose of enhancement of fairness in presentation of scientific theories for the legislation.

The ACLU's alignment of plaintiffs included several Protestants, Roman Catholics, and Jewish officials. The experts called to testify were nationally recognized authorities on religion and science. The main contention was that the equal time statute promoted Protestant Fundamentalism and that Creationism could not be separated from its religious roots.

The Arkansas Attorney General, Steve Clark, countered that Creationism was indeed scientific and based his case primarily on the principle that competent scientists did accept Creationism. Clark's scientific witnesses were largely ignored by the press because they lacked the national reputation of those for the plaintiffs. Scientists who accepted Creationism with a minimum of religious motivation included William Scot Morrow of Wofford College, an agnostic who described Creationism as a theory on the cutting edge of science; Wayne Friar of King's College; Margaret G. Helder of Brock University in Canada; Donald Chittick, formerly of George Fox College; Ariel Roth of Loma Linda College; Harold G. Coffin of the Geoscience Research Institute; N. Chandra Wickramasinghe, chair of the Applied Mathematics department at University College, Cardiff, Wales; and Robert Gentry, visiting researcher at Oak Ridge National Laboratory. These defense witnesses fared poorly under cross examination, in part because Judge William R. Overton refused to accept the state's contention that the source of a theory did not invalidate its standing as a scientific theory.[17]

In early 1982 Judge Overton released his decision that the Arkansas law was unconstitutional. He relied upon the published statements of religious faith of those involved in drafting the law and the court testimony of those sponsoring the legislation.[18] He then noted that the definition of Creationism in the law was essentially identical to a literal interpretation of Genesis. He finally noted that Creationism did not hold the respect of the scientific community since it was not published in the scientific journals. He rejected the defense contention that evidence against evolution was evidence for Creationism.[19] His siding with the scientific community's rejection of Creationism as science was regarded by the Creationists as evidence of bias.

The effect of *McLean v. Arkansas* was widespread. In April of 1984 the Texas Board of Education rescinded its decade-old "anti-dogmatism" regulations.[20] A bill in South Carolina was withdrawn, one was not submitted that had been planned in South Dakota, bills were not introduced in Missouri and Kansas, and were left in committee in Arizona. Bills in Florida were delayed and never passed.[21]

The Louisiana Case

The Louisiana situation was different. While the ACLU argument was essentially the same as in Arkansas, in Lousiana the defense was different for a variety of reasons. A longer debate had preceded the enactment of legislation in July of 1981 with academic freedom more prominent in the debate and religious motivation inapparent. Wendell Bird was named a special assistant attorney general and led the defense. Bird contended that a different definition of Creationism made religious motives for the legislation a false argument. Bird also filed suit (*Keith v. Louisiana*) seeking compliance with the act, so the two cases proceeded at the same time. An effort to repeal the act before it went to trial passed the state Senate but failed in the House.[22]

The federal court actions were complicated. The *Edwards v. Aguillard* court initially withheld a decision until resolution of the Keith suit. The Keith court sought to avoid the issue by saying it was a Louisiana dispute between the Senate and the state agencies and therefore, ought to be resolved in the Louisiana courts. Keith was dismissed. This forced the Aguillard court to consider the case. On November 22, 1982, without a trial, Judge Adrian Duplantier ruled that the Louisiana constitution gave authority to the state Board of Education to "supervise and control" the schools. The legislature, having authority only to "establish and maintain" the schools, had usurped the Board's authority making this one of the most sweeping judicial limitations of legislative authority in history.[23]

Upon appeal of the ruling, the federal appellate court certified the issue of state constitutional law to the Louisiana Supreme Court which rejected the federal trial court's interpretation of the limited power of the legislature. The scientific and religious questions were remanded by the federal court of appeals to the federal trial court. On January 10, 1985, Judge Duplantier entered a summary judgment against the Louisiana act as unconstitutional on essentially the same basis as the Arkansas decision, that is, that it promoted religion. The state appealed the decision to the U.S. Court of Appeals for the Fifth Circuit, which affirmed the summary judgment in a close eight-to-seven vote. The minority opinion at the appeals level led the state to believe that it might have a chance, so the case was appealed to the Supreme Court.[24]

The Supreme Court heard argument on December 10, 1986, and rendered the decision in *Aguillard* on June 19, 1987. The Supreme Court found the act a violation of the establishment clause of the First Amendment because it lacked a secular purpose. The Court by a seven to two majority found that the act served to advance a particular religious belief. This finding appeared to be strongly influenced by the "Friend of the Court Briefs" by 72 Nobel Prize recipients and 24 of the major science organizations in the United States.[25] Furthermore, the Court reasoned that the Act introduced religion unnecessarily by advancing belief that a supernatural being created humankind; thus, it was patently unconstitutional.[26]

Enthusiasm for pursuing further court tests of the equal time concept has receded for the time being. A major factor is the high cost to the states of litigating these cases. Arkansas spent over $1.5 million defending its law, including $400,000 paid to the ACLU for their costs in fighting the legislation. and Louisiana spent over $400,000.[27] These figures have caused other legislatures to hesitate before passing Creationist legislation. This does not mean that Creationism has disappeared, however, for Creationism involves both social and religious forces. The firmly held position of the Creationists will not disappear just because the Supreme Court has ruled that it is inappropriate for teaching in the public schools. This decision may well force additional Fundamentalists to place their children in private schools where Creationism will be taught. Furthermore, just as the Courts excluded prayer and Bible reading from the schools only to see it continue in isolated places, it seems likely that Creationism will continue to be presented in some schools across the country.

This chronological summary leads to intermingling the two issues the Creationists have raised. The first issue is the constitutionality of teaching Creationism. Clearly, three decades of litigation have led to the establishment of evolution as legitimate science to the satisfaction of the courts on the basis of expert testimony. It cannot be excluded from the public schools. Also, it is now clear that statewide mandated teaching of Creationism will be regarded as the establishment of a particular Protestant interpretation of the

Bible in the schools and will not be allowed. The exact limits of private conscience have not been established, for in Kentucky the individual teacher may instruct about Creationism if the teacher wishes.

The result of litigation upon the second issue of what may and what must be included in textbooks is less clear. The courts have traditionally avoided mandating curriculum and appear reluctant to begin with this issue. The Federal court decisions appear, however, to be causing the Creationists some difficulties on the state level; thus, they will be forced to emphasize local action. For example, in 1985 the California Textbook Commission rejected all the middle school science textbooks as having an inadequate discussion of evolution. The textbook publishers were thus forced to treat evolution delicately to avoid the dogmatism restriction while still having to please the scientists. They were allowed to meet the problem with supplementary materials for California in 1985 and 1986.[28] New Board of Education guidelines clearly favored evolution but opposed dogmatism in presenting it, which left unclear the degree of tolerable criticism and whether presentation of Creationism was possible. The textbook problems are not finally resolved nationwide.

The Creationist Influence Upon Textbooks

In addition to the legal battles over textbooks, other actions were taken. Parents were largely successful from Scopes to Sputnik in keeping evolution out of textbooks. However, after Sputnik they began to lose control to educational professionals. Since Christians feel a very strong obligation to teach their children Christian precepts, and since there is a deep antipathy toward the secular segment of society that ignores faith and seems willing to use the schools to replace church and home, the parents were aroused to action. The textbook crusade must be viewed as part of a larger movement aimed at reducing general social deterioration. Activism in the political arena is no longer strange to Fundamentalists, but even if wrong they are hardly a threat to the continuation of a free society, guilty of censorship and a new Nazism, as some have indicated.[29] This is certainly a failure on the part of the opposition to regard the traditional rights of the minority in America to seek to influence the majority. Thus, they have sought to influence the schools through the textbooks.

The success of the Creationists in affecting the textbook selection process stems from two factors: the local control of education through school boards and statewide selection of schoolbooks in two of the larger states that happen to have sizable conservative populations. Local control of education stems from the historic development of our school system. When high schools began to proliferate in the late 1800s, they were a development of civic pride, not a statewide legislatively-supported movement. They were financed from local taxes, and therefore the municipality exercised control. This tradition is now ingrained by 100 years of development. It has worked amazingly well, although some social planners regard it as anarchistic. The lack of state or federal control has allowed immense amounts of innovation and experimentation. If innovations proved unhappy, as in the case of open classrooms in the early 1960s, the damage was local and fairly easily undone. If the innovation worked well, for example, the Middle School concept, it soon spread.

On the other hand, in the case of science education, the consequence was rather haphazard. There was little possibility of the schools being brought into line to support national objectives such as wartime or Lyndon Johnson's war on poverty. With increasing state financing in some states and federally mandated and financed programs, especially those for the handicapped, coordination has increased in recent years. The National Education Association has also contributed significantly to the standardization of American education, frequently assisting with improved teaching strategy and efforts to improve quality. Less admirable to the Creationists is the frequently expressed humanism that the organization endorses.

An area of increased coordination has been in textbook purchases. Several states have moved to central textbook committees that determine which books will be used in statewide school systems. Usually seven are selected in a given subject, with autonomy exercised over which of the seven is selected for purchase in the local school system. Two of the largest states, Texas and California, have centralized textbook selection. That is why these states figure so prominently in influencing textbook publishers, since over 15 percent of the national market is in these two states. The centralized selection process also is obviously vulnerable to pressure groups including the Fundamentalists. Those two states and the Fundamentalists in them thus have achieved national prominence.

As indicated previously, the event that precipitated the involvement of the Fundamentalists with textbooks was the publication of two curriculum programs by the National Science Foundation. The Biological Sciences Curriculum Series became a national problem. The particular issue with the BSCS texts as far as the Fundamentalists were concerned was not evolution *per se*, but the fact that the scientists seemed to have deliberately sought to antagonize the religious community by focusing upon Man as an animal and upon his evolution. This was particularly offensive to the religious community that believes Man was a special creation who differs dramatically from the animals.

Once the BSCS series of texts was published, the opposition began almost immediately in Texas. Under the leadership of pastor Reuel Lemmons in the Church of Christ denomination, strong pressure was brought to bear on the Texas Board of Education not to approve this text. The result was initially inconclusive. Lemmons was supported by Mel and Norma Gabler, who have become the most prominent textbook watchers in the country. In 1969 they succeeded in convincing the Texas Board of Education to exclude the BSCS series from the approved list. Shortly thereafter, the Gablers founded Educational Research Analysts, which provides witnesses at public hearings, speakers, and analyses of specific textbooks upon request. In May of 1974 they were instrumental in securing an amendment to the Texas Education Policy Act which required the identification of evolution as a theory which was not factually verifiable and only one of several explanations of origins.[30]

Before that controversy died it was further aggravated by the publication of *Man: A Course of Study* (MACOS), a text designed for the social sciences, psychology and sociology. Again it was based on evolutionary principles, with the blurred distinction between Man and the animals as part of the problem, and with the additional element of relativism in the area of beliefs and attitudes, which were based upon sociological studies rather than theological perceptions of right and wrong. As sociologist Dorothy Nelkin has observed, the lack of scientific rationality was evidence of technological decadence from the scientific perspective while the dominance of scientific rationality was moral decadence from the Fundamentalist perspective.[31]

The power of the Fundamentalists can be noted by simply following their legal progress. Even before the publication of BSCS and MACOS, the issue was already drawn in California, where under the leadership of the conservative Max Rafferty, the California School Board approved guidelines which specified that Creationism had to be taught if evolution was taught. The 1973 rules specified that evolution had to be taught non-dogmatically, a result of the suit by Kelly Segraves. These rules, after an immense controversy, were eventually revised and a compromise reached. A committee of Creationists suggested changes in approximately thirty textbooks, and the scientists representing the biology teachers agreed.

In addition to the Segraves in California and the Gablers in Texas, other organizations joined the textbook controversy. The Heritage Foundation, which originally drew its funding from the brewer Joseph Coors, opposed federal funding of textbook projects. Leadership Action, based in the nation's capital, sought to increase citizen participation in textbook selection during the 1970s. The Council for Basic Education opposed some NSF curriculum efforts.[32] We must note in caution that none of the Creationist efforts to secure equal time (or balanced treatment) is censorship, as Nelkin implies.

Activities by lobbying groups led the Oregon School Board to rule in September 1973 that school libraries must have Creationist resource materials, and that teachers were to encourage students to weigh both sides of the debate. In most other states in the mid-seventies, however, efforts were not made on a statewide basis but on the local level. In Ohio a statewide organization assisted in making Creationist material available to local libraries and school libraries.

In 1976 the extensive effect of Creationism appeared with the issuing of a history text, *Streams of Civilization*, by the Creation-Life publishing arm of the ICR. The text affirmed that all of history has occurred in 10,000 years, most geological formations are the result of a world-wide flood, humans and dinosaurs were contemporaneous, and all races and civilization began in Mesopotamia, in clear contradiction to recent studies that appear to show central Africa as the most probable origin of early Man.[33]

Alternative Education for Creationists

Another way that parents have sought to control their children's education has been through the formation of private alternative schools in locations where they have been unable to achieve their objectives. The motive was seldom the teaching of creation, but the same Fundamentalism was frequently at play, and these schools almost uniformly are Creationist in their approach to both history and science.

Perhaps the most famous local confrontation was in Kanahwa County, West Virginia, where parents marched in the streets in 1974 to protest godless education. An ugly split developed between urban Charleston and the rural parts of the county. Both sides were willing to resort to force to have their way. Charleston ultimately adopted a balanced treatment policy, introducing Creationism into the schools, as had Dallas, Texas, and Columbus, Ohio.[35]

More recently the Creationists appear to be losing ground. In 1984 following the revision of the Texas *Guidelines*, and in accord with a select committee on education recommendations, the twenty-seven-person Creationist-dominated elected board was replaced by a fifteen-member board appointed by the governor. While the board was thus removed from the immediate influence of the voters, a Creationist governor could quickly restore the Creationists to power.[36] That same year California, New York and Florida formed the "textbook cartel for excellence" to counteract the influence of Texas in "dumbing down" the content of science textbooks through the removal of information about evolution.[37]

Losses for Creationists continued when governor Bob Graham and his cabinet, who sit as the state school board in Florida, approved twenty-two biology texts of which Creationists disapproved because they included evolutionary material.[38] In December 1985 California rejected all junior high school life science textbooks because of inadequate coverage of evolution. Following minor revisions, the books were accepted in 1986 despite continued objections from the scientific community about errors and misconceptions presented in the books.[39] In early 1989 the Texas Board of Education adopted new guidelines that required information about evolution in biology textbooks, whereas previously they had required evidence contrary to evolution. The new regulations did require instruction in any other reliable scientific theories.[40] Still other evidence that Creationism is losing ground nationally is that opponents have decreased coverage of Creationist activities. An example is that *The Humanist* discontinued its "Creation/Evolution Update" page in 1986.[41]

At this point the Creationists have lost the issue of mandated teaching of Creationism and appear to have passed the apex of their power in influencing textbook writing. An aroused scientific community appears as powerful a lobby with publishers as the Creationists. We may expect, however, continued pressure at the local level to voluntarily introduce Creationism on an individual basis.

Opposition to the teaching of Creationism in public school classrooms on the part of Christians who are not Creationists should not be construed as opposition to Christians voicing their concerns about anti-biblical and anti-Christian teaching in the schools. Every Christian has the same right as non-Christians in voicing their concerns. We must, however, choose the best issues and the best biblical interpretation possible.

The debate over Creationism in the public schools also does not address the issue of whether Christian children should be in public schools or private schools. That is a difficult debate beyond the scope of this study. Of concern, however, is the teaching of a false science in the Christian schools. That is a practically unaddressed issue in Christian circles, the Creationists having become so dominant. One possible outcome is that there will be a decline in Christians entering the scientific fields, leading to further separation of science and faith.

In a context of broader social issues the Creationists have appealed to a basic resistance to science. It is persistent because more than just Creationists regard science as a threat to traditional values. More than just Creationists resent the authority of scientific expertise, especially when scientists abuse their authority. More than just Creationists fear a compromise of egalitarian and plural-istic views in America. For the time being Creationists are content for equal time in contention with what they regard as the pernicious atheistic tendency of evolution, yet the very campaign to introduce Creationism into the public schools indicates fascination with the power of public education and the scientific community. The Bible, literally interpreted, teaches that education, especially religious and moral, is the responsibility of the parent and the religious community (the Church in our day). The Creationists are in es-sence granting that the state is the appropriate educational author-ity by seeking to direct what the state teaches regarding creation.

At this time it is difficult to perceive how successful Creation-ists will be on the local level. Accreditation of Christian Heritage College in California and Liberty University in Virginia as well as other Creationist schools insures a continuing supply of Creation-ist public school teachers. The growth of the National Association of Christian Educators, which is supportive of Creationism, also indicates increasing influence on the local level.[42] In many com-munities Creationists are a vocal minority and in some cases a majority. In larger communities, groups of scientists and other citizens concerned about the separation of church and state have formed opposing groups. The scientists are deeply concerned about the attempt to resolve a scientific debate in the public arena. If Creationism is finally forced to face evolution on its scientific rather than political merits, it will fail. If science, however, ignores the public moral attitudes, it may also find that its resources disappear. In the following chapter we will trace some of the difficulties that have arisen as scientists have battled Creationism.

Evolution as an Alternative

Strategies of the Evolutionists

The effort by scientists to defend evolution from the Creationists and to prevent the introduction of Creationism into the public schools has generally been conducted maturely. There are, however, some excesses in the defense of this biological theory that reflect metaphysical presuppositions which create a philosophy of evolutionism. Evolutionism is the infusion of the theory with a goal orientation and mindset that the biological evidence does not support. In a lively fight, questionable reasoning, dubious arguments and enthusiastic rhetoric can creep into otherwise sound arguments. This has happened in the creation/evolution debate.

Scientists hold a very powerful position in society through their role in higher education and their contribution to technological advances which have resulted from scientific discovery. Scientists who have power in the academic community have developed a useful relationship with the government that has resulted in extensive support for the science. In addition, the research and development programs of American industry provide a source of employment and finances about which previous generations could only dream. However, if this support and influence is threatened by environmentalists or Christians the scientific community can be roused to action. If unthreatened by religious activists, most scientists are indifferent to Christianity, especially in the workplace.[1]

A few of the responses to the Creationist threat have been emotional. Some responses in journals such as *The Skeptical Inquirer* and *Creation/Evolution* are sarcastic, belittling, and unprofessional. Especially subtle are statements that impugn the motives without refuting the scientific fallacies of the Creationists, such as suggesting that Creationists propagate facile sophistry and are only superficially dispassionate.[2] Some statements in opposition to Creationism are expressed in such personal terms that they appear to say more about the author than the opponent. Some "scientific" responses to Creationists may be influenced by the responder's reactions to rigid religious parenting and overly simplified childhood religion that never developed. Some responses appear not to have outgrown the colorful sarcasm that decorates university classroom lectures, but which most scholars abandon when they write professionally.[3] Some responses seem to come from beliefs inherited from strong personalities on university campuses, without serious evaluation of the underlying philosophical presuppositions. The key to understanding these responses is the recognition that they are not the result of reasoned defenses of faith being defeated by reasoned critiques of that faith. Such criticisms are partially rooted in the emotions.

Some responses to Creationism are motivated by simple self-protection. When the Creationists sought to secure federal legislation mandating equal grants to Creationists, even though their numbers are much smaller, it took little effort to arouse scientists against that legislation. A second example of self-protection is the adoption of the either/or dichotomy proposed by the Creationists. Some scientists have accepted the "only two choices" hypothesis on the basis that if the Creationists are roundly defeated, the residual influence of Christianity in our society will also be reduced.

Errors of Historical Interpretation

The conflict between Creationism and evolutionism has been heightened by those who have accepted the outmoded warfare hypothesis to explain the relationship of science and religion. In this context, Creationism is seen as just the latest battle in a long war. The parameters of this perspective were set by the strongly anti-Catholic position of John William Draper's *History of the Conflict Between Religion and Science* and Andrew Dickson

White's *History of the Warfare of Science with Theology in Christendom*, which included the Protestants as enemies as well.[4] The warfare interpretation went essentially unchallenged in American historiography until the 1930s, when the Puritan clerics were discovered as the chief supporters of the new astronomy and other scientific achievements in New England.[5] Despite historical studies which have demonstrated that urbanization, immigration, prosperity and indifference had more to do with religious decline than science, the military metaphor has persisted. The Scopes trial and the renewed Creationist debate have strengthened warfare interpretations, but the trend is at least away from reading the current debate into the past.

A counter-balance to the warfare hypothesis has been the theme that Protestantism gave rise to science. Sociologist Robert K. Merton proposed in a study of the members of the Royal Society of London that Protestantism was crucial to the rise of science.[6] His thesis has been criticized for ignoring earlier Catholic scientists and for distorted definitions of religious affiliations within the Royal Society. The thesis has not been destroyed. More recently apologists such as Reijer Hooykaas and Eugene M. Klaaren have developed this interpretation, but most historians no longer attribute the rise of science to Protestantism alone, and Stanley L. Jaki especially wants to include the Catholics. The moderating effect of this interpretation has been to support rejection of the warfare thesis.[7]

Errors of Logic

Scientific apologists in the debate with Creationism have fallen into a number of identifiable intellectual and logical errors. Probably the most egregious error is the belief that scientists are free from philosophical presuppositions.[8] While recognizing the Creationist commitment to theistic presuppositions, scientists frequently fail to recognize their own commitment to exclusive cause and effect relationships as the ultimate control in the physical world. Geologist Robert J. Twiss reminds scientists that science is a philosophy with rules that limit it to reproducible phenomena that "...inherently have the potential to be disproven." He also suggests that religion is a philosophy that can admit either Creationist or evolutionary understandings, creating at least three alternatives.[9] Although logical positivism is not so prominent as it once was among scientists, many still reject all metaphysical statements as empirically unverifiable and consequently meaningless, the latter being what the theist denies.

Some scientists such as Linus Pauling could be described as naturalistic humanists, seeking to retain values but making the comfort or common good of humanity, as defined by the scientist, the measure of the value of all things. It is easy to present evolution as an anti-theistic secular system that necessarily results from research, rather than as a philosophy that is properly labeled "evolutionism." An associated difficulty is that some scientists seem unable to differentiate magic and superstition from theology and philosophy. As they reject superstition, they assume they are free from metaphysical assumptions within naturalistic philosophy.

Another problem arises when scientists know their science better than their theology. Naïve theological interpretations by scientists are as prevalent as literalistic ones by the Creationists. C. Leon Harris, in his discussion of pre-scientific understandings of nature, states that taking woman from man's rib expressed the dependence of women upon men, an obviously outmoded concept, and therefore evidence of the negative cultural influence of the Bible.[10] This interpretation ignores the positive cultural position of the biblical ethos compared to its cultural environment in the ancient world. This particular criticism of the Creationists is built upon exactly the same kind of literal interpretation of the passage of which the Creationists are accused.

Evolutionists are sometimes intemperate in language, unnecessarily deprecatory toward Christianity and the biblical record, simplistic in stating the positions of the Creationists, and guilty of sweeping dogmatism when the complexity of their subject does not lend itself to facile explanation to the public. Reason, if it is indeed powerful, will persuade with reasonable argument. There is no excuse for distortions such as the suggestion that Creationists' final authority is the King James Version of the Bible, that Darrow made a monkey out of Bryan at Scopes, or that all Creationists are propagandizers who do not hold their views sincerely. Other rhetorical claims are that Creationist writings are fatuous, that their goal is totalitarian, that they burlesque civil rights, and that they are irrational, incompetent and silly.[12] Such name calling is unbecoming the seriousness of the genuine issues at stake in the debate. Harris's suggestion that we need not take the Bible seriously if any errors at all are found in it could hardly be applied to any portion of the history of science. Nor does his recitation of errors display anything other than a literalism that exceeds that of the Creationists.[13] It certainly conveys that some scientists are not free from their own emotional and metaphysical commitments.

Yet another type of problem arises from arguing against beliefs that no one really holds. The simplest case is the setting up of "straw men" that are easily demolished—distortions of Creationist thought that are not representative, but are easily refutable. C. Leon Harris suggests that the Creationist commitment to catastrophism would mean there would have to be a great number of Edens to replenish the Earth after each catastrophe, since there is evidence for a great number of catastrophes.[14] Similarly, complex positions are collapsed into a simple one. Many evolutionists write about "special creationists" as if they were all of one mind.[15] There is, however, a vast difference between a Benjamin B. Warfield, who accepted evolution except for the human soul, and the six-day Creationist who believes that each species was a special act of creation. Another distortion results from the claim that all the geological strata add to scores of kilometers, although in any one location fifteen is perhaps the limit of their depth. In refuting flood geology the claim is then made that the Creationists have to account for the scores of kilometers.[16] In reality they only have to account for what is actually deposited at any one site. This is not to suggest that the Creationists could account for even 15 kilometers of deposits, but nothing is gained by exaggerating the problem for the Creationists. Yet another problem is the substitution of non-equivalent terms in a chain of evidence. Again, the NAS demonstrates very clearly the systematic evidence for change through time, but then with a mere dash "descent with modification" is substituted for "change through time." These are not equivalent, and the subtle attempt is to substitute the "how" it happened when the evidence was for "what" happened.[17]

While many of these errors of logic and distortions of opponents' positions are innocent blunders, there is also a dispute in the realm of philosophical presuppositions. The nineteenth-century secularization of science went beyond the removal of superstition or magic from science. Elimination of God altogether was a goal. In the eighteenth century, Deism removed God as a participant in the natural world, but all evidence of God was reinterpreted to demonstrate that he was an unnecessary hypothesis in a natural explanation of the universe and its inhabitants. A few scientists are committed to the proposition that God as an actor in creation is impossible if science is true. The contention here is that God was too easily removed, not on the basis of evidence, as the National Academy of Sciences believes,[18] but because the theist did not present intellectually sound alternatives as Mark Noll, the historian, suggests.[19] A further problem was that the theistic evolutionists of the late nineteenth century tended toward Lamarckian explanations. With the defeat of Lamarckism the scientists applied the defeat to theistic evolution as well. Clarifying the relationship between secular and theistic evolution requires a closer look at how Darwinism triumphed in the United States.

The Acceptance of Darwinism

The advent of Darwinism was extremely significant, and many intellectual historians regard the *Origin of Species* as one of the two most significant books of the nineteenth century, the other being Marx's *Das Kapital*. Both have contributed to dramatic change in the world since the 1850s. The *Origin of Species* provoked a major intellectual uproar primarily because one of the grand accomplishments of science up to Darwin's time had been the banishment of the idea of spontaneous generation (the idea that life could arise without antecedents). The fixity of species was a position for which scientists had fought, one which Christians thought compatible with the Bible. Thus, when Darwin challenged the fixity of species, he faced formidable scientific as well as theological opposition, for even though he was not advocating the older idea of spontaneous generation, he was attacking the major weapon against it.[20]

There were other concerns as well. Adam Sedgewick, one of three outstanding geologists in the world at the time, had been a teacher of Darwin, yet he dismissed the new theory as materialism whose objective was not science, but rather an anti-religious effort to make men independent of the Creator of the universe. The apparent "trial and error" nature of evolution was in contrast to the design that would be expected of a wise and good creator. Survival and selection in a blind process potentially reduced even Man's free will. Theists who adopted evolution attempted to soften it by proposing the presence of design in God's shaping of what variations were possible. Evolution was interpreted as a means to a purposeful end.[21] The Princeton theologian Charles Hodge would have none of that; he simply called it atheism. Thus, religious opposition to the materialistic and anti-religious potential of Darwinism was present from the beginning.

Despite the opposition, however, there was also an environment more accepting of evolution for a variety of reasons, including the fact that evolution was "in the wind" at the time. For many intellectuals the late nineteenth century was a period of disintegrating orthodoxies. The "old ways" appeared inadequate to cope with the dramatic changes wrought by science, technology, democracy, large-scale capitalism, urbanization, immigration and a host of other new developments. For these scholars, Darwinism posed an explanatory means that promised liberation from metaphysical and theological dogma. This was the responsive audience that immediately began to apply Darwinism as a metaphor far beyond the bounds of botany—to linguistics, anthropology, sociology and some parts of political theory and philosophy.

Darwinism was quickly adopted because it was compatible with another trend, the secularization of intellectual life. Prior to the nineteenth century, theology permeated all areas of intellectual thought save for that band of French scholars led by Denis Diderot and Voltaire. During the last century, however, there was a growing desire to replace theology with mathematics as the queen of the sciences. Theology, at best, would become merely a branch of human thought on a par with history or philosophy, rather than the foundation for all. This transition allowed many Christians to adopt evolution without abandoning the Creator, for they reasoned that God simply adopted this particular means for accomplishing his creation. Unlike the skeptics, however, the Christians who adopted evolution did not perceive it as random and directionless, but rather as directed toward beneficent ends.[22] The idea of progress was strong in the late nineteenth century, and Darwinism was seen as a visible proof of the legitimacy of the concept of social progress.

Darwinism was also quickly accepted because it was relatively simple, almost awesome in its power to explain what had previously been largely disjointed observations. Moreover, it was supported by examples Darwin had meticulously gathered over twenty years.

Three years before he published the *Origin of Species*, Darwin finally communicated his plan to someone outside his immediate circle of friends. That person was Asa Gray of Harvard University, who had been a longtime correspondent of Darwin and who frequently provided botanical specimens for him. Once the book was published, Gray did not ardently support it, since he believed his support might increase resistance; rather, he sought to give it a fair hearing. He could do this as editor of *Silliman's Journal*, one of the major American scientific journals.[23]

The theory was strongly debated in Boston for more than a year, primarily because Louis Agassiz disputed it with his own theory, which was that species arose in many places at approximately the same time. This was a more extreme kind of special creationism than that held by most Christians, and since Agassiz had no mechanism to explain how his species arose simultaneously in multiple locations, he gradually lost the day. Following this debate in Boston, the *Origin of Species* was widely reviewed and discussed in other periodicals. Many negative reviews appeared, with some concentration of these in the religious periodicals.

Even so, the popularity of the theory grew, and with Harvard setting the pace, evolution was introduced into the botanical and zoological classrooms on college campuses. The organizational power of the theory was apparent, and soon textbooks were rewritten with formats that followed to some extent the patterns of evolution.[24] By 1880 the hostile *Presbyterian Observer* could find only two American naturalists who did not accept evolution. Asa

Gray's *Elements of Botany* was one of the most popular high school texts in that field. He simply moved the Creator behind the scenes, with evolution the "immediate instrument" for speciation.[25]

Geological Adoption of Darwinism

Although geologists had recognized the great age of the earth for over four decades, they did not readily adopt Darwinism. They had accommodated great age into their interpretation of Genesis and felt less compulsion than the botanists and zoologists to adopt Darwinism. Not until the late 1870s and 1880s did geology textbooks begin to reflect Darwin. Edward Hitchcock, the president of Amherst, and James Dwight Dana of Harvard were primarily responsible for this delay. However, by 1874 Dana converted to theistic evolution and revised his textbook.[26] This theistic evolutionary position was the one adopted by most Christians during the last quarter of the century, but that changed very rapidly.

The complete commitment of geology to evolutionary principles was the work of Louis Agassiz's students, among whom was the Harvard geologist Nathaniel Southgate Shaler. Shaler was a practicing field geologist for Massachusetts, Kentucky and the Geodetic and Coastal Survey. In addition, his skill as a lecturer caused his basic geology course to have the largest attendance of any course on the Harvard campus. His upper level classes attracted numerous students, and he trained more geologists than any other person in the United States during the three decades surrounding the turn of the century. Shaler was a believer in a naturalistic theology and avowedly evolutionary.[27] Another Agassiz student, Joseph LeConte, wrote a strongly evolutionary high school geology text which replaced Dana's more moderate one in popularity.

In addition to influencing teachers and textbooks, Darwinism also penetrated the general scientific community. In the late nineteenth century American science had essentially two branches: geophysics and natural history. Geophysics was largely promoted through geological surveys and publications of the state governments and through various exploratory geological surveys of the national government in the western territories. The emphasis of the state surveys was upon practical usefulness, that is, upon timber and mineral resources, but the chemistry of soils and the physics of mountain building also received a great deal of attention. By 1900 the geological, chemical and geophysical developments were regarded as equal in quality and quantity to that done in Europe.

Abandonment of Theistic Evolution

The abandonment of theistic evolution for anti-evolutionary Fundamentalism by conservative churches is difficult to trace. Ronald L. Numbers has assisted with an excellent study of G. Frederick Wright which follows this Oberlin professor's movement from a position as Asa Gray's foremost associate in spreading theistic evolution to a place as the leading Fundamentalist opponent of science. Wright appears, however, to have retained belief in natural selection and limited interventions by God to the end of his life.[28] The pressure that pushed Wright and presumably other Christians into a Fundamentalist position, according to Numbers, was the attacks upon the Bible by the literary critics and the openly antagonistic and sometimes arrogant attitudes of the scientists. As the critics posed their questions, many Christians moved from regarding the Bible as infallible on matters of faith to believing the Bible infallible on everything, or invalid altogether. The cultural perspective of the Bible and its common-sense descriptions of natural phenomena were totally lost in this trend. A second cause for the demise of Darwinism among the most conservative Christians was the general scientific doubt about the theory of evolution, centering primarily upon the inadequacy of explanations for the cause of variations. The extreme Creationist position flowered in the hands of George McReady Price.

Natural history was even more widely pursued because it lent itself to accomplishment by the amateur. The professionalization process was well underway, but it was not complete during this period and lagged somewhat behind that of the geophysical sciences. The American effort was largely non-quantitative, with the natural historians somewhat less committed to the experimental method than their European counterparts. Darwin contributed to changing that by bringing order out of chaos and giving linear direction to the classification system. In addition, he stimulated research in physiology, microscopy and biochemistry. Amateur dabbling in geophysics and natural history rapidly turned into recognizable science.

While Darwinism gradually dominated late nineteenth-century science, resistance to Social Darwinism raised some concerns about the theory. Peter Bowler, an historian, states that the primary concern was whether natural selection was an adequate explanation for evolutionary change. Bowler finds four major themes in the alternative theories to Darwinism proposed between 1880 and 1920: theistic evolution, a revised and updated Lamarckism (the inheritance of acquired characteristics), orthogenesis (evolution under the influence of unknown organismic forces), and mutationism. There were even positions holding different combinations of these non-mutually-exclusive alternatives. These scientific alternatives were not unrelated to the social and religious opposition as well, for even a serious scientist like Thomas Hunt Morgan believed the mutation theory made it possible to avoid the "...dreadful calamity of nature, pictured by the battle for existence."[29] None of these alternatives was sufficiently comprehensive and powerful to reduce the hold Darwinism took upon the scientific community.

Illustrative Current Issues

Since theistic evolution has had few well-known spokesmen after 1920, and since the Creationists have moved to the forefront, the evolutionists of a strongly anti-Christian persuasion seem to believe that they have won, even if politics and the courts have been slow to catch up. One reason, however, why the Creationists continue to receive a public hearing is because there are some genuine difficulties with evolution.

One problem is the issue of the "God of the gaps." Some scientists have accused Creationists (and other Christians) of merely using God as an explanation whenever there is a void in the scientific explanation of things. Some scientists believe that everything does have a natural explanation and that God therefore is ultimately unnecessary. As a consequence, they expect the gaps in knowledge to close in the future, and God will be squeezed out as this happens. Sometimes this does appear to be the process, for in the last century G. Frederick Wright expected Darwin to continue to be unable to explain the origin of variations. First genetic theory provided a foundation for neo-Darwinism, and more recently microbiological research has discovered the mechanisms of genetic variation. This particular niche for the "God of the gaps" has closed with time. Wright did at least encourage Christians to avoid theological causes until all rational causes had been exhausted.[30]

A second major difficulty is the traditional argument from design; that is, that the order and cohesion of nature implies an organizing God. By selectively choosing data, a few scientists have made a case for the random and statistically chaotic nature of the universe. To most students of scientific literature, however, the universe seems filled with examples of the consistency of natural law and dependable causality for cosmic events. For most observers, these seem to point more to design than to randomness. Some source for the perceived design is necessary. Simply appealing to an internally directed evolution through such phrases as "nature's design," or "the creatures of nature," is not sufficient. For most observers it is not clear at all that there should be a direction to evolution or a design in the consequences of that evolution, without intelligence selecting the direction or providing the design. Asking that the complexity of the universe appear naturally is an act of faith. Some scientists appear to attempt to meet the problem of directedness by rejecting the idea that evolution is directed toward anything, especially anything superior. Others have simply dismissed this issue as "the old argument from design," which does nothing to refute it. During the past century the most ardently defended replacement for design has been the concept of rationally-based progress. Science, in this view, opened the way to technological improvement, which in turn enhanced Man's environment (health, longevity, leisure). Improvement in the quality of life leads to a spiral of improvement or progress. However, world wars and ecological disaster have made progress seem more illusory than it was in the past.

Having rejected God and a designed universe, many scientists have adopted mechanistic views of the universe. Philosophical Naturalism explains all observed phenomena in terms of physical elements and processes. Such a mechanistic philosophy remains popular since it makes the physical world intelligible, although it is weak in accounting for any meaning to life and seems to undergird much of the current opposition to Creationism. In a mechanistic system different physical conditions would result in different outcomes, but the assumption is that specific conditions give determined results. One of the most popular recent deterministic theories is that of the behavioral psychologist B.F. Skinner, as expressed in his book *Beyond Freedom and Dignity.*[31] Skinner attempted to demonstrate that all matters that appear to be the result of choice are really predetermined since all choice is based upon preconditioning. While Christians grant the partial truth of conditioning, deterministic views go counter to both the Christian faith and practical experience in the areas of choice and responsibility. Aesthetics and the development of human values seem to refute thoroughgoing deterministic systems of thought. Deterministic views are thought by both evolutionists and Creationists to be subversive to the argument from design. It remains, however, presumptive to assume that discovery of a physical cause for an event dismisses God. This assumption is a leap of faith.

None of these philosophies—materialism, mechanism, or determinism—avoids a dependency upon metaphysical reasoning on the part of its proponents. Their very multiplicity indicates the difficulty of finding integrative answers to the large questions, given the very restrictive rules that science places upon itself.

A third current issue arises from those few who make science their religion, a religion known as "scientism." While the number who have made some sort of "atheistic humanism" their religion is genuinely small, a larger number pursue pseudo-religious intellectual constructs that parallel many elements of the Christian gospel. For example, there are some who cannot accept God as the creator, yet who are aware of the "aura of mystery" that infuses the evolution of the cosmos. There are some who could not accept Christ as a redeemer, yet who look to the discovery of superior civilizations on other planets to assist us in ending war, hunger and the other ills of our planet. There are those who expect "future science" to provide eschatological hope and usher in the Millenium. There are those who reject old-fashioned moral law, whose primary law has become "whatever is possible must be investigated." These elements portray a larger indebtedness to theology and the reassurance of religion than some scientists would care to admit.

There are, however, more substantive scientific issues than the above. Some of the heat of debate in the geological area is because of some weaknesses in the scientific case. One reason the Creationists are believable to many people is that the geographical and stratigraphical location of some fossils finds is haphazard. The geological journals contain a small editorial undercurrent of frustration concerning the fact that many geologists inadequately locate their finds. Some of the more bitter complaints suggest that as much as 50 percent of all fossil finds are improperly located and can contribute little to evolutionary chronology.

A second major reason that Creationists win converts is that scientists are not always candid about radiometric dating. While the Creationists ignore the corroborating indexing by different radiometric methods, as well as the astronomical evidence, it is also true that the scientists tend to ignore anomalous results and the failure to even date things at all. The issue of priority seems to push some scientists into taking the most extreme ancient date. In the especially sensitive area of dating hominid ancestors, it appears that many finds are never dated radiometrically, but are dated on the basis of anatomical variation. The suspicion appears to exist even among scientists that the most ancient remains are least likely to be dated objectively. For the best case to be made for evolution we should be able to expect the greatest care in the dating of fossils and human remains.

Scientists clearly believe that evolution is a fact, meaning that ever since life appeared millions of years ago, it has assumed increasingly complex forms with the passage of time. There is no doubt that this has happened, for the evidence clearly indicates it. Moving from this description to the assertion that evolution is the means of bringing about the observed changes is an inference, not a fact. It may well be a true inference, but it remains an inference. On the other hand, Creationists claim that there is no evidence for evolution, meaning that genetic change followed by natural selection is inadequate to account for the observed fossil record. Even if the gaps in the fossil record are closing, there are some persistent problems. The transition from single-celled protozoa to marine invertebrates seems beyond the reach of the fossil record, although that does not necessarily make this transition false.[32] The transition from carbon-based proteins to living cells seems to be more remote from duplication in the laboratory than it was twenty years ago as additional knowledge has accumulated about what must take place. There also seem to be few transitional fossils closing the gaps between phyla and classes, especially for the fish.[33] This, however, should be small comfort to the Creationists, since there are transitional forms from fish to amphibians and reptiles to birds, which means the gaps do not match up with the points of creation of Genesis One.

Biology is not the only science in which evolutionary problems are glossed over. Much is made by anthropologists of homologous bone structure as an evidence of common ancestry; but it could also mean common function rather than common ancestry. The long-sought common ancestor of man and the ape has still not been found. The impression persists that new discoveries populate the gaps of known species more than they fill the transitional forms needed. The theory of punctuated equilibrium, the idea that long periods of stasis are followed by periods of geologically rapid change, is an admission by the biological community that species are stable and gaps persist in the fossil record. In the light of these problems it would seem that a more balanced account of the evidence for macro-evolution does need to be made.

Cosmological Issues

In a materialistic system, matter is of greatest value. For some cosmologists the issue is not value, but rather that an eternally existing universe would reduce the necessity for the existence of God. This has been a difficult conception to give up. The best cosmological evidence at present, however, is that the universe had a very definite beginning, before which nothing can be deduced. Further, the second law of thermodynamics implies an eventual decay or heat death of the universe or at least an ending. The idea of a beginning and an end sounds too much like the linear Christian view of the universe, so various scientists have sought a way out. In the early 1950s astronomer Fred Hoyle and his associates developed the theory of continuous creation, that hydrogen molecules originated spontaneously in deep space to replenish the energy of the universe and keep the evolution of stars going. Hoyle openly stated that he desired a more philosophically pleasing system than one with a beginning and an end. The increasing evidence for an expanding universe, however, has caused nearly all cosmologists to accept the "Big Bang." Ernst Opik, George Gamow and John A. Wheeler have suggested that the universe oscillates, expanding and then contracting to be born all over again in yet another Big Bang. This would again allow an eternal universe, but it is hardly a scientific theory since it cannot presently be verified.[34] For this reason there is a continuing search for "dark matter," which would allow enough matter in the universe to contract again and allow for an oscillating universe.

The Origin of Life

Alternatives to Christian views of God's creative act in the origin of life have also been proposed. Around the turn of the century, the Swedish Nobel prize winning chemist, Svante Arrhenius, proposed a theory of panspermia, the idea that life on Earth resulted from seeding by spores that were transported across space. The discovery of ultraviolet radiation that would kill any life forms in space ended this particular speculation, but the proposal of an English physicist, Norman Lockyer, that life was initiated on the planet by life-bearing meteorites, has enjoyed a somewhat greater vogue. It has been reinforced by the discovery of organic molecules in some meteorites. Even were such a discovery that life came from space to be verified, that would only push the origin of life to an ever more remote location where it would be impossible to discover how it occurred.

The complexity of life also raises problems. The severe difficulties in replicating life beyond the simple amino acids raise serious questions with the spontaneous origin of life as an adequate explanation, because of the high order of complexity and the contradictory needs at different stages in the process. An excellent explanation of these problems may be found in Jim Brooks' book,

Origins of Life.[35] The mounting difficulties in explaining how life originated on this planet need not make Christians uncomfortable about believing in an interventive intelligence who initiated the process. Pejoratively calling this special creation does little to cope with the philosophical and theoretical difficulties. At the same time the evidence for the process of evolution is sufficiently strong that it is apparent that God did not necessarily create each living or extinct specie.

As scientific research moves toward the remote past, the evidence becomes more scarce and problematic in interpretation. The study of origins in some sense is as much historical as scientific, since it is unrepeatable and not generally subject to experimentation. Thus, some "scientific" statements are inferential and subject to the presuppositions of the one engaging in the study. As a consequence, there is wide variation in the interpretations of the evidence among the scientific community when discussing origins. These issues of scientific epistemology have been dramatically exploited by the Creationists to imply that the scientific method and scientific results are undependable and frequently erroneous. While the unreliability of science is exaggerated by such claims, it remains true that in the area of origins interpretations of data are frequently governed by presuppositions rather than by the evidence itself.

The obvious key for the Christian is whether God is eliminated *a priori* or not. If God is excluded by the philosophy of science, no evidence for his existence and participation could persuade. The assumption is that God could not intervene and still have a logically consistent, law-abiding universe. The greatest difficulty Christians face in confronting those who ardently support evolution is that while the claim is that evidence and logic forced such a conclusion, the reality is that the exclusion of God was not driven by the evidence but by personal preference. Attempts to explain immediate scientific causation as if that exhausted all that is known, that purpose and design are irrelevant, is simply scientific metaphysical imperialism and not the appropriate stance for the scientist. All forms of human knowledge have limitations.

Must We Choose Creationism Or Evolutionism?

The beginning point for the theist is acceptance of God's existence, and his role as the Creator of the universe. While evangelical Christians may well accept randomness within a probabilistic framework in the creation process, the Christian rejects the idea that God has no role. The universe is a purposeful consequence of God's will carried out by both natural and supernatural means. Some scientists say that we ourselves impose the order, essentially creating God in our own image. The Christian inverts this assertion and states that we can see the order because we are created in God's image. The evangelical Christian affirms that there is purpose in Man's existence and that we have dignity and worth, not as the epitome of the natural order, but because of the image of God in us, the spiritual side of Man. The Christian further affirms that science and religion need not be at war, are not totally separated from each other in influence upon one another, and are not mutually exclusive just because science tends to deal with the how and when, theology with the why. Christians believe in an orderly creation that provides a meaningful basis for scientific study—creation by a dependable God who is not arbitrary, capricious, whimsical or deceptive.

These affirmations are supported by extensive theological study, historical evidence, rational consistency and personal experience, all of which attest to the efficacy and validity of the Christian message. All Christians affirm the reliability of the Bible in spiritual matters, a revelation of God's working relationship with Man. The Bible clearly claims God as an active Creator, but despite Creationist claims, it is not explicit about the methods of that creation.[1] Many Christians affirm that God has used natural means to accomplish the bulk of the creative process, and special creative acts are few and only occur at specific strategic points. The most widely agreed-upon points of intervention across both the centuries and across denominational lines are the introduction of life into the universe and the soul into man, which distinguishes him from being a mere animal. The evangelical Christian position is not an "unconstrained whimsy of an omnipotent God," as William J. Bennetta has asserted,[2] but well reasoned and logically and internally consistent.

Proper Interpretation

There is a widely-accepted, hermeneutically sound method of interpreting the Bible. The discussion of Creationist failings in chapter five pointed to the most significant of these principles: attention must be devoted to the historical and spiritual context of the creation passage to avoid the Creationist mistake of mythologizing Genesis One as science and thereby making it theologically bankrupt. Literary type must be attended to as well as the intention of the author, the message for his own day, and the timeless message that may be contained in the passage. In the "Foreword" to Henry Morris's commentary upon Genesis, the statement is made that of the 20 or so commentaries currently in print, his is the only Creationist one.[3] The author of the foreword apparently misses the clear irony of Morris' minority status and recent departure from the traditions of biblical scholarship. His twentieth-century technocracy confuses the concepts of truth, factuality, and literalness, collapsing them all into one and confusing both the meaning and the richness of the biblical record. In effect, he, as the father of Creationism, claims that the poetic and the symbolic, because they are not literal, cannot be true. Few scholars of literary method would so want to limit the variety, depth and richness of the great literature of the Bible.

Probably the most widely discussed word in the Bible outside of atonement and righteousness is the word "day." Biblical scholars for centuries have written learned discussions on the variety of meaning of this particular word. In a language like Hebrew where every word has three basic letters and the vowel sounds are not included in the written language, the historical and literary type become a dominant factor in determining the meaning. Some commentaries have estimated that there may be as many as a hundred different meanings in the Bible for the word "day." Among these multiplied meanings are many non-literal ones implying periods or epochs. During the last two centuries as the great age of the universe has become apparent, biblical scholars nearly unanimously have accommodated the concept of age by viewing the days of Genesis One as epochs.[4] The Creationists thus represent a recent departure from traditional Christianity in their insistence upon literal 24-hour days. But this entire discussion rather misses the point if the purpose of Genesis One was something other than a scientific account of the creation of the universe.

Interpreting Genesis One

Determining the purpose of Genesis One is strategic to interpretation. Creationists claim that the Bible, when it deals with origins, is a reliable scientific document in its explanation of the processes of creation. The problem is that Genesis One may well not be discussing the processes of creation at all. Just as science does not explain all that there is in the thought life of Man, the Bible also does not explain all. While the Bible deals in depth with significant issues of life, death and relationships, it is not exhaustive in its descriptions of the natural world any more than it is exhaustive in its dealing with every conceivable social or spiritual issue. Some Creationists will even grant that the primary purpose is non-scientific, but that if it touches on the natural world it has to be true. Obviously the sanctity of truth does not extend to our interpretations of the Bible, and if we clearly misinterpret a passage to make it scientific we are indeed on dangerous ground. The contention here is not that the Bible is untruthful, but that it is directed toward a different purpose and says little about the processes that God used in creation.

For centuries prior to the advent of the Creationists, Genesis One has been understood as a semi-poetic apologetic or teaching passage regarding the polytheism of the cultural environment of the ancient Hebrews. Even Fundamentalist G. Frederick Wright, who contributed to the original series on *The Fundamentals*, accepted the truth of this particular statement.[5] The purpose of Genesis One is to establish that no created feature of the Earth or of the heavens is worthy of worship. One by one the passage considers the deities of the surrounding culture and finds them the creations of the one true God, who alone is worthy of worship. The passage serves as an introduction to God's actions toward people, based upon his nature as the Creator. The passage is not about science (the nature of nature), but about the nature of God. Turning it into a message about science trivializes the majesty of the meaning of God's action in history and makes science much too important an enterprise. God is narrowed to the terms of a scientific world view. Science at best can corroborate faith, but it cannot authenticate faith.

A very significant issue in interpreting Genesis One and Two is the order of events.[6] In Genesis One the creation is a waste and void. Light and darkness exist. The dry land, grass, seeding herbs and fruit trees appear on the third day. On the fourth day the Sun, Moon and stars appear after the plants dependent upon them have already been created. Aquatic life and birds appear on the fifth day, and man and beasts on the sixth. In the second chapter the order is very different. First man appears, then trees and then beasts and birds. If the order were to be accepted in both accounts, they would contradict one another. The purpose of the semi-poetic Genesis One is the issue of worshipping false gods, and not the order of creation. The purpose of the storytelling nature of Genesis Two, where the players in the plot are introduced according to importance, is explaining why sin exists—as a consequence of God's gift of free will. Ignoring these different purposes and literary types leads to this conflict in order and consistency.[7] Creationists have proposed a variety of *ad hoc* explanations for the problems of order. The arrival of plants before the Sun is dismissed as no problem if they were there only one twenty-four-hour day before the arrival of the Sun. A second Creationist suggestion is that the primordial light mentioned on the first day was diffused by a cloud canopy over the whole of the earth, so that plants could have had sufficient light even before the advent of the Sun. These suggestions are plausible only if the 24 hour days are granted despite the overwhelming scientific evidence against them.

More importantly, however, focusing upon the order of the six days of Genesis distorts our understanding of the structure of the passage the author used to convey his thoughts concerning the power, authority and uniqueness of God. As many commentators have pointed out, the author clearly has a cyclical structure in mind to express the wholeness and completeness of the creation. Note the following arrangement:

1) Light / Darkness   4) Sun / Moon and stars

2) Firmament / Water   5) Aquatics / Birds

3) Land / Plants   6) Beasts / Man

There is actually evidence of multiple structuring in the passage. Note that there are two and only two creations each day. The second set of three days populates the creations of the first three days, which provides a sense of fullness or completeness appropriate to this Hebrew context. The objective of expressing the fullness of creation by God is reinforced by the use of twelve acts of creation, twelve having a typical Hebrew meaning of completeness or "all that there is."[8] A further emphasis upon the wholeness of creation comes from the contribution of the seventh day Sabbath, which gives the sense of integration or meaning to the whole, a meaning traditionally attached to the number seven in Hebrew culture. Rather than being merely a scientific recounting of the order of the steps of creation, the deeper theological meaning of this passage is one of wholeness and completeness. This meaning is emphasized by the repeated evaluation that it was good, and when completed it was very good. However, while the creation is indeed marvelous, it is still not worthy of worship, in whole or in part, which is the emphasis of Genesis Two. It must be noted that while Genesis One does not present a linear order of creation, it is not thereby a false or erroneous passage. It is merely fulfilling a meaningful and truthful purpose of relating God to the creation.

The semi-poetic nature of the passage has caused some Roman Catholic commentators in the past to allegorize the passage and make other extreme departures from the literary structure and theological content of the passage. The near poetic rhythm of Genesis One in Hebrew and the use of parallelism have been frequently noted by commentators, but the passage is neither pure poetry nor pure parallelism; rather, it is a blending of the two. The passage is unique in the Bible, and it apparently served a special purpose. That purpose seems clear from the setting in the Pentateuch and from other Old Testament passages. One of the besetting problems for the Hebrews was to establish their loyalty to God in the face of continual temptation to relapse into the worship of the gods of the surrounding cultures. Over and over in the Pentateuch, Joshua and Judges, the Israelites are reminded of the mighty acts of God on their behalf. They are repeatedly admonished to teach their children these basic facts. In a society where writing was the province of only the few, the story of the great events of the past was handed down in stylized memorable form. That appears to be exactly the function Genesis One played. It was a simple catechism used for the purpose of demonstrating that the gods of the surrounding cultures were not worthy of worship, because God created everything.[9] This interpretation is reinforced by the passage in Isaiah 40:12-13 and 21-23 where the Israelites are asked if they did not know from "The Beginning" that God alone was worthy of worship.

Who has measured the waters in the hollow of his hand,

or with the breadth of his hand marked off the heavens?

Who has held the dust of the earth in a basket,

or weighed the mountains on the scales

and the hills in a balance?

Who has understood the mind of the Lord,

or instructed him as his counselor?...

To whom, then, will you compare God?

What image will you compare him to?...

Do you not know? Have you not heard?

Has it not been told you from the beginning?

Have you not understood since the Earth was founded?

The implication is not just "have you not known?" from times past, but "have you not known?" from a particular passage that expressed the beginnings. That passage is Genesis One, the catechism of the Hebrews concerning polytheism. Isaiah was reminding the Hebrews of the catechism they were supposed to have learned, and as a consequence reminding the modern reader of the meaning of Genesis One.

The accuracy of this interpretation of Genesis One is reinforced by its place in the larger theme in the Old Testament of establishing the worship of God. Many elements of Hebrew worship were borrowed from surrounding cultures but turned to a different purpose. Much of that difference was provided by the well-known Hebrew linear view of history, as opposed to the annual fertility cycles that tended to dominate the worship of surrounding cultures. The Hebrews had a developmental approach to history, with history having a goal and Man having a destiny. That goal is that every knee should bow and worship the Creator. So Genesis One presents the other gods: gods of light and dark in day one, the local sky and storm gods and the river fertility gods of the Nile on day two, the harvest fertility gods on day three, the Sun and Moon gods and goddesses on day four, the worship of birds and serpents on day five, and the bestial (Baal) gods and self-worship on the sixth day. As Conrad Hyers has said, the issue was idolatry, not science; syncretism, not natural history; theology, not chronology; faith in God, not theories of origins.[10]

The above interpretation of Genesis One thus shows that there is not only little said about the order of creation, but there is nothing said about the means or time the process of creation took. The manner of God's participation in creation is neither a matter for rejection by the most extreme scientists nor for being overly-specific (as some Creationists do), but a matter for investigation and thought. The use of a process such as evolution need not be a problem for the Christian so long as the consistency of natural law, the intelligibility, orderliness and design of the universe, the sense of directionality in the evolutionary process, the meaning of history, and the purpose of the entirety are kept in mind as evidences of God's wisdom and his interaction with his creation. Christians need not accept the excessive claim of the thoroughgoing materialist that any supernatural intervention means that the totality of the natural law is invalidated. Rather, the Christian claims that the supernatural intervention of God—in creating the soul of Man for a moral purpose, for example—need not invalidate the general applicability and relevance of the natural law. Most Christians no longer perceive design as did the early nineteenth-century theologian Paley; he believed that each species was perfectly matched to its environment by means of individual acts of creation. Also, design need not be limited to homologous structures that appear in many different species, but which serve different purposes. These do not imply that the Creator had only a limited number of patterns that he could use. Most Christians now see the evidence for design in the harmony of the laws by which the universe functions, and which have governed and still govern the course of change within that universe.

Science and Interpretation

Current science need not be viewed as undermining the role and significance of God.[11] The Bible affirms the goodness of the physical world, which makes it worth detailed study. The physical world is not an illusion, nor is it irrelevant to human concerns. Genesis One implies that God spoke the universe into existence, an indication of the source of that great burst of energy that we have come to call the Big Bang.[12] Genesis also implies that God brought the solar system into being, but it does not indicate whether this was by fiat or by natural means. Thus, we find in the Scriptures no final answer to the question of whether the solar system is unique, or whether there are many solar systems as most scientists assume, but for which there is little evidence.[13] Genesis also indicates that God initiated life, allowing the Christian to perceive the cause of this existence. Again, the Bible does not indicate whether the creation was by fiat or by natural means, leaving us with no final biblical answer to the question of whether life on other planets exists, as most scientists assume, or whether life is unique to this planet. Finally, the Genesis account indicates that God created Man in his own image. Since God is a spirit, the image of Man must be the spiritual part of the soul. Since the creation is from the dust of the ground, one possible implication is that the soul was imparted to an already developed humanoid creature. Some scientists have attempted to prove that Man is no different from the animals; that is, he possesses the same faculties, developed to a greater degree. Christians have always emphasized the difference of Man, indicated by the aesthetic sense and the development of systems of values.

These four points of intermediation may be dismissed as just another form of the old "God of the gaps" argument; but they do point out that Christians do not necessarily see God as individually creating each species or each star, but rather may have used natural processes to accomplish the task. Predictably, science will continue to have difficulty in finding naturalistic explanations for the evolution of the universe at these points. If God did indeed mediate, the methods of science will simply be unable to bridge these points.

The Limitations of Science

For the evangelical Christian, the scientific enterprise is extremely important. Science, however, is not all that there is. The study of evolution can quickly become Evolutionism when the scholar moves from exploration and explanation of physical and biological phenomena into extrapolation, where evolution is perceived as having its own internal guidance system (creative evolution) and a predetermined destination apart from God's design. Then evolution has adopted a modified orthogenetic position (driven by some force toward a determined end) and has become metaphysical, hence non-scientific.

While such evolutionism does exist, it is doubtful that it strikes at the infrastructure of society any more than any other sin that places Man as all there is without need of God. Evolutionism is undoubtedly a contributor to the general drift of society away from commitment to Christ and the Church, toward ignorance and indifference toward God. The occasionally shrill voice of Creationism, pressing society to adopt its "science" without its commitment to Christ, will not solve the societal damage that neglect of God brings. The tactic has, however, elicited the very organized opposition that Creationists claimed antedated their organization. Unfortunately, the opposition the Creationists have aroused may well damage the efforts of all the Church to express in a more effective manner the relationship of God to his universe.

In addition to evolutionism a further problem for scientists stems from the very restrictions that science places upon itself. Scientists refuse to ask some of the important questions because the answers cannot be verified or replicated. Science is further unable to answer many questions, even some that it legitimately raises. When the claims of ultimacy for science do appear, we may be assured that the scientist making that claim has stepped over into the province of the metaphysical. Even the descriptive facts of science are not directly apparent; they are mediated to the scientist by his personal beliefs. The intellectual milieu in which one works and the structures of one's mindset have their effect upon the scientist as well as the theologian.

At its worst, science has its pathogenic side, just as religion does. The lust for power and the sense of greed can infect scientists as well as anyone else. Anyone who has worked in the laboratory, on a university campus, or read the history of science is well aware of the overweening pride, jealousy and competition that can infect those working in the same field. In the effort to "succeed," some scientists have "cooked" their data; that is, they have adjusted the actual results to fit what they were supposed to get. Evidence exists that Mendel's genetic results are too good to be true. The field of cancer research has been especially prone to falsified research data because of the large amounts of money available for research. To keep those grants coming, scientists have, on occasion, resorted to falsified results.[14] The selling of personal philosophy as popular exposition of science as Carl Sagan and John G. Taylor have done is another example. The need for moral and intellectual integrity on both sides of this debate is apparent.

Evangelical Christians can interpret the Bible with integrity and accept the non-speculative results of the scientific community with equanimity. We need not be afraid that science will destroy the faith. We can affirm the long tradition of retaining the ties between the natural revelation and the special revelation, viewing the universe as a result of the action of God.

Christian Obligations

Christians still have some significant obligations with regard to both the Creationists and the evolutionists.[15] We need to avoid the restrictive biblical interpretation of the Creationists that forces rejection of legitimate evidence for the great age of the universe. This evidence does not conflict with the Bible which, when properly interpreted, gives no strict chronology of events. We must similarly avoid the excessive literalism of the Creationists that in effect makes God a liar, since he created physical evidence for great age which supposedly conflicts with the Bible. We must be willing to accept the indefiniteness of life, understanding that there are few final answers.

Fair evaluation of the conflict over Creationism requires serious academic and intellectual effort. We must note that evolution is a viable method for God to use in the creative process, even though it may be unable to account for certain crucial steps in that process. We need not unnecessarily replace material causation and natural law with miracle in order to be faithful to the nature of God. While rejecting the extremes of special creative acts that Creationists impute to God, Evangelical Christians are indeed "special creationists," believing that God can and does act in connection with his universe. Being a special creationist in this broader sense means we live in a composite world, illuminated by both science and the Bible, by both the physical and the spiritual.

Scientific Disarray

One reason that Creationism has seemed so plausible to some is that evolutionists have been in disarray. There is dissatisfaction with gradualism as an explanation for the transition from specie to specie, since it is not entirely what the fossil record implies. Punctuated equilibrium has made significant progress. Creationists who have quoted David Raup (Chicago's Field Museum) and Stephen J. Gould ignore that the genetic role in accelerated speciation as it is used by Gould does not support Creationist beliefs concerning the fixity of species or "kinds." The Creationists also misinterpret the meaning of "chance" (which means following the laws of probability) to mean "accident." They must also misinterpret "neo-catastrophism" as a label applied to punctuated equilibrium (which means many localized events, or a sequence of major events) to mean one world-wide flood. They also assume that evolutionary stasis refutes evolution, whereas it only disputes gradualistic evolution, and that only on a species-by-species basis.[16]

Another evidence of disarray is the growing influence of Cladism (Clade comes from the Greek "*klados*," meaning branch). Cladism is a taxonomic method that organizes life on the basis of objectively measurable physical similarities. While microbiological measures of divergence are used to indicate approximately how long ago the divergence appeared, Cladism concerns itself little with why or how the divergence took place. The Cladists claim they are expressing the known facts about biological divergence without the speculative extrapolations of traditional neo-Darwinism. Cladism provides little encouragement for Creationists, for it supports concepts of nested patterns of resemblance that unify all of life (what we would expect from common ancestry), but it does not necessarily support God's creation of each specie separately.

There is also serious frustration among scientists with the intractability of the origin of life problem. Books like that of Thaxton, Bradley and Olsen, that clearly state the difficulties with the current formulations for how life arose, are receiving an open hearing, even if the theistic orientation of their conclusions is rejected. Their work is having some impact.[17]

Another disorienting development was the publishing in 1981 of research that apparently supported the inheritance of acquired immunological tolerance, if the acquisition was during the neo-natal period. The significance of this apparently Lamarckian result was great enough that the editors of *Nature* urged extreme caution in interpreting the results and called for independent confirmation.[18]

Christian Responsibility

In the midst of this unusually active time of flux within the evolutionary scientific community, Christians must be especially careful to avoid jumping on the various anti-Darwinian bandwagons that come along, whether it be punctuated equilibrium, Cladism, a new Lamarckism, or the less defensible mysticism of Arthur Koestler, the clearly pseudo-scientific musings of Immanuel Velikovski or the search for Brontosaurus in the Congo.[19] The Scriptures, properly interpreted, do not require an anti-evolutionary stance, and as a consequence it is appropriate to hold a decision in suspense.

Christians must aid scientists in recognizing their own metaphysical assumptions. This is probably most effectively done in private conversation with them. But where the issues are more serious, the appropriate arena for the resolution of conflict between science and religion is in the professional journals and conferences. These issues are inappropriately resolved in one-sided debates in non-juried journals, or in the classrooms of America. Christians also need to distinguish carefully when the issues are amateurish social pronouncements by scientists versus the actual science they practice. Many adept laboratory scientists have only rudimentary sociological and philosophical understandings, since their training in these disciplines often ended at a relatively elementary level.

Christians have an obligation under American law to keep the metaphysical debate out of science classrooms. Creationism is not science and should not be science. Cutting creation loose from its origins in the Bible does a disservice to the overwhelming importance of the doctrine of creation as a part of the whole of Christian theology. The theology of creation must not be separated from the rest of theology; to do so weakens doctrine and removes the essential purpose that Creation, the Fall, and redemption give to history. Those enthusiasts for science who have built the Creationist movement must interact with theologians to avoid the excesses of poor interpretive methods. They have strayed into making science too important by trying to make the Bible a Western technocratic document, rather than letting the Bible speak its own message.

Finally, as Christians, we must all avoid arrogance.[20] Little is to be won by thinking we know it all. However unsatisfactory this may seem, the relationship between science and religion is not always clear. We must accept partial answers, improve understanding, and accept our debt to the past as we approach the scientific and religious problems of the present.

Conclusion

Very probably this book will persuade no naturalistic interpreter of evolution of the error of excluding God. Similarly, it is very unlikely that any Creationists can be persuaded to amend their thought patterns and processes by the arguments presented here. However, for the majority of Christians who are in neither of these groups, the intention has been to provide some reassurance that there is a viable way that accepts the reliability of the Bible and the results of science. There is a long tradition of theistic interpretations of evolution to which the majority of Christians in times past have subscribed. Even though accepted, the positions have been vague, poorly defended, ignored by the scientific community, and they generally have not been prominent in intellectual circles. One purpose of this particular historian is to state as clearly as possible the legitimacy of the mediating position of theistic evolution and to encourage scientists and theologians to state the scientific and theological cases more comprehensively.

All Christians have a stake in the successes and failures of the Creationists, who cannot be allowed to hold the field as if they express the only Christian position. The primary concern is that they will ultimately fail because they reject not just the theory of evolution, but solid evidence from geology, biology, physics and astronomy as well. They do an injustice to God by rejecting the physical evidence of his universe when it conflicts with their interpretation of the Bible. The Creationists claim that evolution is an interpretive theory posing as scientific fact, but they themselves represent a theory of biblical interpretation posing as fact.[21] This cannot ultimately be a successful effort.

Contrary to what the Creationists claim, atheism is not the natural and inevitable outcome of the acceptance of the evolutionary process. Evolutionary thought in biology and geology is not a sufficient philosophical or metaphysical foundation for the rejection of the existence of God and his participation in the creative process. A flexible position of interpretation of both the Bible and the results of science is most likely to produce satisfactory results in the long run. A first principle is that the natural revelation and the special revelation do not conflict, but interpretations of them will. Those conflicts must be evaluated and studied for what they reveal of the motives of those who propound them.

There is a biblical and scientific position for the majority of Christians, a responsible way that needs more exploration, exposition, and encouragement. The truth is more difficult to discern than either the Creationists or scientists would have us believe. We may continue to hope with the frontier Presbyterian minister of the 1870s, Oren Root, that conflict will result in "...broader truth and a higher and wider outlook for humanity."[22]

Notes

CHAPTER I

(1) "Scientific Creationism" will be defined by its beliefs in chapter two. It is a theory about how the Bible should be interpreted. For now, the scientific Creationist may be informally defined as one who seeks scientific data in support of a recent creation (10,000 years ago) of the present cosmos. This special group of people will be cited as Creationists with a capital C throughout this work. In attempting to establish that the doctrine of creation affects most other doctrines, Henry Morris claimed in *The Genesis Flood* that one could not have an adequate belief in the sovereignty of God unless one believed in the universality of the Genesis flood [Henry Morris, *The Genesis Flood* (Philadelphia: Presbyterian and Reformed Publishing, 1961), xix]. In the book *Scientific Creationism* he further claimed that if the Bible and Christianity are accepted as true in any sense, the geological ages must be rejected altogether [Henry Morris, ed., *Scientific Creationism* (El Cajon, CA: Master Books, 1974), 255]. Clifford Wilson indicated that the validity of Christian faith is questionable if it does not begin with origins [Clifford Wilson, *In the Beginning God...* (Grand Rapids: Baker Book House, rev. ed., 1975), 9]. This strong belief in the importance of a recent creation stems from the Creationist perception that evolution is responsible for many of the ethical, moral, philosophical and even theological ills of the present age.

(2) Charles E. Hummel presents a recent and clear summary of the variety of positions among those those seeking such a synthesis. See Hummel, *The Galileo Connection: Resolving Conflicts Between Science and the Bible* (Downers Grove, IL: InterVarsity Press, 1986).

CHAPTER 2

(1) "Division on Creation," *The Christian Century* 99 (September 29, 1982): 951.

(2) "Division on Creation," 951. This contrast between Protestant and Catholic also appears in a Roper/*This World* poll of seminary professors in which 31% of the Protestant professors had reservations about evolution, but only 2% of the Catholic professors did. See Martin E. Marty, "No Radicalism Here: Faculty Survey," *The Christian Century* 103 (August 18-25, 1986): 844.

(3) Kim McDonald, "Pervasive Belief in 'Creation Science' Dismays and Perplexes Researchers," *The Chronicle of Higher Education* 32 (December 10, 1986): 6-7, 10.

(4) The journalist Tim Stafford calls this a difference in "culture," but the components that initiate that difference are philosophical and educational. Stafford, "Cease-Fire in the Laboratory," *Christianity Today* 31 (April 3, 1987): 18.

(5) The political activities of the New Religious Right are extensively and critically analyzed in A. James Reichley, *Religion in American Political Life* (Washington, D.C.: The Brookings Institution, 1985), Samuel S. Hill and Dennis E. Owen, *The New Religious Political Right in America* (Nashville: Abingdon, 1982) and Robert Booth Fowler, *A New Engagement: Evangelical Political Thought, 1966-1976* (Grand Rapids, MI: William B. Eerdmans Publishing, 1982).

(6) Michael Zimmerman, "The Creationists' Appeal for Freedom of Speech...," *The Chronicle of Higher Education* 33 (April 1, 1987), 43.

(7) Conrad Hyers, "The Fall and Rise of Creationism," *The Christian Century* 102 (April 24, 1985): 411.

(8) Hyers, "The Fall and Rise of Creationism," 411.

(9) Richard Bube, a Christian critic of Creationism, indicates that in numerous writings Creationists express their belief as the most basic of Christian beliefs, which places them at the center of the battle against Satan. "Science Teaching in California," *Reformed Journal* 23 (April, 1973): 3-4.

(10) There are many works on religious toleration during the period after 1600 A.D. Three helpful works are Sidney Hook, *Religion in a Free Society* (Lincoln: University of Nebraska Press, 1967), Jay Newman, *Foundations of Religious Tolerance* (Toronto: University of Toronto Press, 1982), and J. Philip Wogaman, *Protestant Faith and Religious Liberty* (Nashville: Abingdon Press, 1967).

(11) There are many good sources for the study of this controversy. From the Fundamentalist side an older but well written one is J. Gresham Machen, *Christianity and Liberalism* (New York: Macmillan, 1923). Also helpful is a more recent study by James Barr, *Fundamentalism* (London: SCM Press, 1977).

(12) Among the many careful histories of the Progressives and Social Darwinism are: Eric F. Goldman, *Rendezvous With Destiny* (New York: Alfred A. Knopf, 1956), George E. Mowry, *Theodore Roosevelt and the Progressive Movement* (New York: Hill and Wang, 1960), C. Gregg Singer, *A Theological Interpretation of American History* (Nutley, NJ: Craig Press, 1978).

(13) Academic freedom issues are discussed in Walter P. Metzger, *Academic Freedom in the Age of the University* (New York: Columbia University Press, 1961).

CHAPTER 3

(1) The influence of Malthus upon Darwin has been much debated by historians and philosophers in recent years. Among the important sources for this discusssion are Phil Diamond, "The Natural Theologians and Darwin," *The Australian Journal of Politics and History* 26, no. 2, (1980): 204-211; S. Herbert, "Darwin, Malthus and Selection," *The Journal of the History of Biology* 4 (1971, 209-217. R.M. Young, "Malthus and the Evolutionists: The Common Context of Biological and Social Theory," *Past and Present* 43 (1969): 109-145; F.N. Egerton, "Studies of Animal Population from Lamarck to Darwin," *Journal of the History of Biology* 1 (1968): 225-229; Peter J. Bowler, "Malthus, Darwin and the Concept of Struggle," *The Journal of the History of Ideas* 37 (1976): 631-651; and P. Vorzimmer, "Darwin, Malthus and the Theory of Natural Selection," *The Journal of the History of Ideas* 30 (1969): 527-541.

(2) Laurie R. Godfrey, ed., *Scientists Confront Creationism* (New York: W.W. Norton, 1983), 18.

(3) Andrew Carnegie, *The Gospel of Wealth and Other Essays*, Edward C. Kirkland, ed. (Cambridge: Harvard University Press, 1965, originally published in 1901), 25.

(4) William Graham Sumner, *Social Darwinism: Selected Essays*, with an introduction and notes by Stow Persons (Englewood Cliffs, NJ: Prentice-Hall, 1963), 157.

(5) See Lester Frank Ward, *Dynamic Sociology* (New York: D. Appleton, 1883).

(6) James R. Moore, *The Post Darwinian Controversies* (Cambridge: Cambridge University Press, 1979), 14.

(7) Theodore Maynard, *The Story of American Catholicism* (New York: Macmillan, 1941).

(8) This brief statement hardly portrays the controversies, complexity and richness of Catholic thought and educational effort. Further understanding may be gained from Ernest Charles Messenger, *Evolution and Theology* (New York: Macmillan, 1932), John Augustine Zahm, *Evolution and Dogma* (Chicago: D. H. McBride, 1896), Zahm, *Science and the Church* (Chicago: D. H. McBride, 1896) and Henri de Dorlodot, *Darwinism and Catholic Thought*, tr. by Ernest Charles Messenger (London: Burns, Oates and Washbourne, 1926).

(9) Moore, *Controversies*, 14. In this major revision of previous historical perspectives Moore concludes that the earliest Christian opponents, in the first decade after 1859, opposed Darwin on the philosophical ground of irregular reasoning. Darwin was not inductive, but posited a new theory to explain facts for which the accepted explanation was the doctrine of creation. This was deemed an inadequate basis for positing a new theory. Moore also suggests that liberal Americans like Henry Ward Beecher, Joseph LeConte and Lyman Abbott confused elements of Darwinism with Lamarckism (that acquired characteristics could be transmitted to offspring) and as a consequence were unaware of some of the implications of Darwinism. They ultimately "...could not coexist with Darwinism because [they] lacked both the consonance with the orthodoxy of Paley and Malthus, and the means of dissonance reduction inherent in Calvinism and Trinitarian doctrines" (16). Moore has higher praise for the orthodox scholars Asa Gray and G. Frederick Wright, who accepted Darwinism but interpreted it not in terms of randomness, but the providence of God, abandoning none of their faith in the process. The consequence for the orthodox was a more clearly understood Christianity.

(10) Galileo, "Letter to Madame Christina of Lorraine, Grand Duchess of Tuscany," *Discoveries and Opinions of Galileo*, translated, with introduction and notes, by Stillman Drake (Garden City, NY: Doubleday Anchor, 1957), 186.

(11) George M. Marsden, *Fundamentalism and American Culture* (New York: Oxford University Press, 1982), 18-20. Examples of those who took an early stance against Darwinism include Francis Orpen Morris, an amateur ornithologist and Anglican rector in West Yorkshire who denied the descent of new species through variation. William Miller, a Scottish pastor, compiled selected quotations that expressed doubts about the mechanism of evolution. T.H. Birks, the Knightbridge Professor of Moral Philosophy at Cambridge regarded evolution as opposed to Scriptures. L.T. Townsend of Boston Theological Seminary dismissed Darwinism as a mere hypothesis, perhaps providing Bryan his source for the same perception. With the exception of Charles Hodge, who concluded that Darwinism was atheism, most of the opponents were not as well known as Darwin's defenders. See David N. Livingstone, *Darwin's Forgotten Defenders: The Encounter Between Evangelical Theology and Evolutionary Thought* (Grand Rapids: Eerdmans, 1987), 131-2.

(12) William E. Phipps in his article "Darwin, the Scientific Creationist," *The Christian Century* 100 (September 14-21, 1983), 809-811, tried to make a case for Darwin as a "scientific creationist," which most closely resembles what I have called a theistic evolutionist. He also argues that Darwin's stance toward Christianity was fairly consistent throughout his adult life from 1838 to 1880. Neither proposition is generally accepted: they appear to represent a misinterpretation of Darwin's desire to avoid conflict with Christians to mean acceptance of the natural theology of William Paley. A more standard, and I believe defensible, interpretation of Darwin's religion is found in John Hedley Brooke, "The Relations Between Darwin's Science and His Religion," in John Durant, ed., *Darwinism and Divinity: Essays on Evolution and Religious Belief* (New York: Basil Blackwell, 1985).

(13) Thomas Henry Huxley, *Darwiniana* (New York: Appleton, 1893), 147.

(14) Marsden, *op. cit.*, 3-8.

(15) Even so careful a scholar as Dorothy Nelkin indicated that *The Fundamentals* not only attacked modernism, but evolutionary theory as well. This is only half the story, more a consequence of her understanding of the sociology of Fundamentalism than a historical fact, for the war against evolution was present only in volume 8 of these early pamphlets. She also sees Fundamentalism as "back woods," which ignores the realities of

Fundamentalist origins. See Nelkin, *The Creation Controversy: Science or Scripture in the Schools* (New York: Norton, 1982), 30. A more balanced view may be obtained from Livingstone, *Darwin's Forgotten Defenders*, 148-153.

(16) Edward J. Larson, *Trial and Error: The American Controversy over Creation and Evolution* (New York: Oxford University Press, 1985), 37.

(17) William Jennings Bryan, "The Fundamentals," *The Forum* 70 (July, 1923): 1679.

(18) Bryan sought to set up a dichotomy between fact and theory. The first was true, the second not necessarily true. In reality, facts (in the sense of observations or measurements) are not immutable and are frequently reinterpreted. Theory is only occasionally patently false and seldom adopted by more than a fringe element if generally regarded as false. In modern terms a theory must be capable of predicting (or postdicting) observable events. This is necessary to accomplish the rejection of theories that lead to unreliable predictions. This principle is commonly referred to as falsifiability. Since the starting point of Creationism is supposedly the one true interpretation (the literal one) of the Scripture, it is not falsifiable without rejecting the truth of the Bible. To protect the truthfulness of Creationism it is then necessary to resort to *ad hoc* adjustments to the system in order to preserve it.

(19) Larson, *Trial and Error*, 49.

(20) Larson, *Trial and Error*, 50-51.

(21) Larson, *Trial and Error*, 58. A full account of the trial appears in John T. Scopes and James Presley, *Center of the Storm: Memoirs of John T. Scopes* (New York: Holt, 1967). Additional sources include L. Sprague De Camp, *The Great Monkey Trial* (Garden City, NY: Doubleday, 1968), Ray Ginger, *Six Days or Forever? Tennessee v. John Thomas Scopes* (Boston: Beacon, 1958), and Mary Lee Settle, *The Scopes Trial* (New York: Watts, 1972). Larson's account is more balanced than some of the others.

(22) Larson, *Trial and Error*, 59.

(23) Larson, *Trial and Error*, 60.

(24) Larson, *Trial and Error*, 65.

(25) Willard B. Gatewood, Jr., "From Scopes to Creation Science: The Decline and Revival of the Evolution Controversy," *South Atlantic Quarterly* 83 (Autumn, 1984): 365.

(26) House Bill 77 (Mississippi, 1926).

(27) Larson, *Trial and Error*, 79.

(28) Maynard Shipley, *The War on Modern Science* (New York: Alfred A. Knopf, 1927), 239.

(29) Larson, *Trial and Error*, 75.

(30) Judith Grabiner and Peter Miller, "Effects of the Scopes Trial," *Science* 185 (6 September, 1974), 832-837. A more personal and individual assessment demonstrating some of the distortions of biology that resulted from the exclusion of evolution is in Stephen J. Gould, "Moon, Mann and Otto," *Natural History*, 91 (March 1982): 4-10.

(31) Maynard Shipley, "Growth of the Anti-Evolution Movement," *Current History* 32 (May, 1930): 330-332.

(32) Otis W. Caldwell and Florence Weller, "High School Biology Content as Judged by Thirty College Biologists," *School Science and Mathematics* 32 (1932): 411-12, 419-20.

(33) Gerald Skoog, "The Topic of Evolution in Secondary School Biology Textbooks, 1900-1977," *Science Education* 63 (1979): 623-7.

(34) George W. Hunter, *Science Teaching at Junior and Senior High School Levels* (New York: American Book, 1934), 32.

(35) Gatewood, *From Scopes to Creation Science*.

(36) Shipley, *War*, 120.

(37) Shipley, *War*, 205.

(38) Shipley, *War*, 123.

(39) Andrew D. White, *A History of the Warfare of Science with Theology in Christendom* (New York: George Braziller, 1955, originally published in 1895) I, 313-5.

(40) Shipley, *War*, 117.

(41) Shipley, *War*, 119.

(42) Shipley, *War*, 189.

(43) Shipley, *War*, 116.

(44) Among the societies formed were the Creationist Society in 1932, the Society for the Study of Deluge Geology and Related Sciences in 1938 and the American Scientific Affiliation in 1941.

(45) Gatewood, *From Scopes to Creation Science*, 308.

(46) Gatewood, *From Scopes to Creation Science*, 371.

(47) Gatewood, *From Scopes to Creation Science*, 372.

(48) Some examples of the more significant works would be Canon Dorlodot, *Darwinism and Catholic Theology*, vol. 1 (1923); J. Arthur Thomson (Aberdeen University) *Science and Religion* (New York: Charles Scribner's Sons, 1925); Kirtley F. Mather (Harvard geologist), *Science in Search of God* (New York: Henry Holt, 1928); E.C. Messenger, *Evolution and Theology: The Problem of Man's Origin* (New York: Macmillan, 1932); Alexander D. Lindsay, *Religion, Science and Society in the Modern World* (New Haven: Yale University Press, 1943), Arthur Rendle Short, *Modern Discovery and the Bible*, 2nd ed. (London: InterVarsity Press, 1949); H.J.T. Johnson, *The Bible and Early Mankind* 2nd ed. (London: Burns, Oates, 1948); P.J. Wiseman, *Creation Revealed in Six Days* 4th ed. (London: Marshall, Morgan and Scott, 1948); Alton Everett, ed., *Modern Science and Christian Faith* (Wheaton, IL: Van Kampen Press, 1948; 2nd ed., 1950); Philip G. Fothergill, *Historical Aspects of Organic Evolution* (London: Hollis and Carter, 1952); Eric Charles Rust, *Nature and Man in Biblical Thought* (London: Lutterworth Press, 1953); and Bernard C. Ramm, *The Christian View of Science and Scripture* (Grand Rapids: Eerdmans, 1954). These demonstrate the wide variety of issues, approaches and concerns of those who sought to minimize the incompatibility of science and religion.

(49) I use the word "renewed" since attacks upon theistic evolutionists were part of the original crusade of the 1920s. The Rev. T.T. Martin, pastor of a church in Blue Mountain, Mississippi and a Bible Crusader activist, said in a speech before the Mississippi House of Representatives,

"The so-called theistic evolutionists refuse to admit that they are Atheists, contending that they believe in a God back of creation; they argue that evolution is God's method, but they put God so far away as to practically destroy a sense of God's [presence] in the daily life and a sense of responsibility to Him. At least, that is the tendency, and since the so-called theistic evolutionists borrow all their facts from atheistic evolutionists and differ from them only in the origin of life, theistic evolution may be described as an anaesthetic administered to young Christians to deaden the pain while their religion is being removed by materialists."

Shipley, *War*, 64. Such attacks were not the norm in the 1920s, but were to be more common in the 1960s.

(50) Joel Gurin, "The Creationist Revival," *The Sciences* 23 (April, 1981): 18. The antiquity of this argument can be seen in a letter from J. Henry Thayer to G. Frederick Wright in which six-day creationism or atheism was regarded as an old style of reasoning in 1884. See Ronald L. Numbers, "Science and Religion," *Osiris*, no. 1 (2nd series, 1985), 631.

CHAPTER 4

(1) The best ones at present include Laurie R. Godfrey, ed., *Scientists Confront Creationism* (New York: W.W. Norton, 1983); Philip Kitcher, *Abusing Science: The Case Against Creationism* (Cambridge: MIT Press, 1982); Ashley Montagu, ed., *Science and Creationism* (New York: Oxford University Press, 1984); Niles Eldredge, *The Monkey Business: A Scientist Looks at Creationism* (New York: Washington Square Press, 1982); Douglas J. Futuyma, *Science on Trial: The Case for Evolution* (New York: Pantheon Books, 1982); Chris McGowan, *In the Beginning... A Scientist Shows Why the Creationists are Wrong* (London: Macmillan, 1983); J. Peter Zetterberg, ed., *Evolution Versus Creation: The Public Education Controversy* (Phoenix: Oryx Press, 1983); The Iowa Academy of Science, Stan Weinberg, ed., *Reviews of Thirty-One Creationist Books* (Syosset, NY: National Center for Science Education, 1984). There are several others of nearly equal value.

(2) See Duane Gish, *Evolution? The Fossils Say No!* (San Diego: Creation-Life Publications, 1979), 34.

(3) This position is expressed in a paper entitled "Evolutionary Theory and the Fossil Record," circulated by the Bible-Science Association of Caldwell, Idaho.

(4) This places them at odds with the biologists for whom morphology has become less important in identifying species as dependence upon more specific evidence has become available, for example, evidence of the stages in the life cycle of the organism, microscopic physiological features, number and structure of chromosomes, biological evidence such as the structure of macromolecules, DNA matching and even behavior patterns are all taken into account.

(5) Joel Craycraft, "Systematics, Comparative Biology, and the Case Against Creationism," in Godfrey, *Scientists Confront Creationism,* 167-9.

(6) See Thomas H. Jukes, "Molecular Evidence for Evolution," in Godfrey, *Scientists Confront Creationism,* 117-122. See also Henry M. Morris, ed., *Scientific Creationism* (El Cajon, CA: Master Books, 1985, reprint of edition of 1974), 51 and 54-58.

(7) Craycraft, 164.

(8) Creationists normally say that all mutations are deleterious and thus evolution is impossible, but Henry Morris suggests that the animals on the ark all hibernated by means of specially created genetic mutations that caused them to migrate to Noah and then sleep once on the ark. See Morris, *The Beginning of the World* (Denver: Accent, 1978), 1-60.

(9) C. Leon Harris, *Evolution, Genesis and Revelations: With Readings from Empedocles to Wilson* (Albany, NY: State University of New York Press, 1981), 112. This claim is forcefully presented (by selective quotation) by D. James Kennedy in his sermon "The Collapse of Evolution," delivered at the Coral Ridge Presbyterian Church, Fort Lauderdale, Florida on September 27, 1981. While nearly every Creationist book raises the issue, one of the most extensive discussions is J. Kerby Anderson and Harold G. Coffin, *Fossils in Focus* (Grand Rapids: Zondervan Publishing House, 1977). They consider all the standard issues—there are no Pre-Cambrian fossils that are antecedent to the complex Cambrian fossils; there are no fossils intermediate to the higher levels of classification, that is, order, class and phyla; and microevolution only occurs within "kinds."

(10) Godfrey, "Creationism and Gaps in the Fossil Record," in Godfrey, 196-7.

(11) Shipley, *War,* 18. See also Linda Mealey, "New Views in Evolutionary Theory," *The Humanist,* 44 (March/April, 1984): 37.

(12) David M. Raup, "The Geological and Paleontological Arguments of Creationism," in Godfrey, 153-155.

(13) Morris, *Scientific Creationism,* 46.

(14) This appears in a mimeographed paper with the title "Summary of Scientific Evidence for Creation." This document was neither paged nor the organization circulating it noted at the end.

(15) In the best scientific tradition of continuous reevaluation of presuppositions, there has been recent geological evidence that has called into question the strongly reducing (non-oxidizing) nature of the early atmosphere. This would complicate current theories of the origin of life immensely. See Charles B. Thaxton, Walter L. Bradley and Roger L. Olsen, *The Mystery of Life's Origin: Reassessing Current Theories* (New York: Philosophical Library, 1984).

(16) That they are now aware of this fact appears in a statement by I. Scott, "If we reject the evolutionary framework then we must also be prepared to have a revolutionary appraisal of the entire scientific tradition." Scott, "History—Influence and Evolution," *Ex Nihilo* vol. 3, no. 1, 21. Cited in Strahan, "Ex nihilo ad absurdum," *Search* 12, no. 7 (July, 1981), 189.

(17) Shipley, *War.* This work is at times quite belligerent as he discusses the actions of Fundamentalists, especially the Bible Crusaders. Shipley was also completely devoted to the outmoded warfare metaphor of Draper and White.

(18) Edmund Gosse, *Father and Son* (London: Heines, 1907), 100.

(19) "Mainstream Scientists Respond to Creationists," *Physics Today* (February, 1982), 54. In addition to Morris, Russel Akridge uses this argument. Morris' clearest statement is in *The Remarkable Birth of Planet Earth* (Minneapolis: Dimension Books, 1972), 61-62.

(20) George O. Abell, "The Ages of the Earth and the Universe," in Godfrey, 36.

(21) Morris, ed., *Scientific Creationism,* 133-36.

(22) Henry Faul, *Ages of Rocks, Planets and Stars,* (New York: McGraw-Hill, 1966), 18. See also Stephen G. Brush, "Ghosts from the Nineteenth Century: Creationist Arguments for a Young Earth," in Godfrey, 65.

(23) J.S. Plaskett, "The Structure and Rotation of the Galaxy," *Publications of the Astronomical Society of the Pacific,* 44 (June 1932): 146.

(24) Morris, *Scientific Creationism,* 131.

(25) A summary of damage done to dinosaur tracks at the Paluxy River site is in Frederick Edwords, "How Creationists Destroy the Past," *The Humanist* 45 (March/April, 1985), 35.

(26) Strahan, "Ex nihilo ad absurdum," 189. Similar accusations of hypocrisy appear in E. Peter Volpe, "'Scientific Creationism' Bill in Louisiana Begat a Feud and a Lawsuit," *Evolution* 35 (1981): 1249.

(27) A favorite Creationist quotation is from Karl Popper, the philosopher of science, who once wrote that evolution was not falsifiable in the same manner as the other hard sciences. Creationists have quoted this as meaning that evolution is not falsifiable, and therefore is not science. They neglect the phrase "in the same manner." Popper stated in an interview that he did not mean that evolution was not falsifiable, only that the approach had to be different. Nils Eldridge and others give examples of specific tests that could falsify evolution. Despite the disclaimer, the Creationists persist in this claim.

(28) *Scientific Creationism* and *What Is Scientific Creationism?* are two books that present a systematic approach to Creationist arguments, but despite being systematic these works present neither a comprehensive theory nor a comprehensive survey of all the areas of science that would have to be reinterpreted if Creationism were true.

(29) American Scientific Affiliation, *Teaching Science in a Climate of Controversy* (Ipswich, MA: ASA, 1986), 20-21.

(30) Also, earlier Creationists had recognized that some of the footprints were faked, and the "best examples" had disappeared. See J.D. Morris, *Tracking Those Incredible*

Dinosaurs and the People Who Knew Them (San Diego: Creation-Life Publishers, 1980), 238.

(31) Frederick Edwords, "Footprints in the Mind," *The Humanist* 43 (March/April, 1983), 31. This problem of evidence was also presented in the Public Broadcasting System's Nova series program on "God, Darwin and Dinosaurs."

(32) ASA, *Teaching Science*, 20-21. See also Frederick Edwords, "Seeing the Light," *The Humanist* 46 (March/April 1986): 33. The footprints also involve the issue of giantism in the first eleven chapters of Genesis and other scattered places in the Old Testament. Some Creationists have interpreted Genesis 6:4, Deuteronomy 3:11 and Joshua 18:16 as referring to men as great as twelve feet tall. See C.L. Burdick, "When GIANTS roamed the Earth," *Signs of the Times* (July 25, 1950), 6 and 9. See also C. Doughterty, *Valley of the Giants* (Cleburn, TX: Bennett Printing, 1971; 6th edition, 1978), 51. See also F. Beierle, *Man, Dinosaurs and History* (Prosser, WA: Perfect Printing, 1977; rev. 1980), 95-8. A skeptical refutation that errs in the opposite extreme is J.R. Cole, "It Ain't Necessarily So: Giants and Biblical Literalism," *Creation/Evolution* 5 (Issue 15): 48-54.

(33) See Gish, *Dinosaurs, Those Terrible Lizards* (San Diego: Creation-Life Publishers, 1980), 1-62. For a refutation see Thomas H. Jukes, "The Creationist Challenge to Science," *Nature* 308 (March 29, 1984): 398. For an unfortunate use of Gish's argument in a Creationist-dependent critique of evolution see Francis Hitching, *The Neck of the Giraffe: Where Darwin Went Wrong* (New Haven: Ticknor and Fields, 1982), 87.

Chapter 5

(1) Edward Norman, *Christianity and the World Order* (New York: Oxford University Press, 1979), 6.

(2) Among the many good books relating to the interpretation of documents one may consult Max Black, *Critical Thinking* (2nd. ed., New York: Prentice Hall, 1952); Joseph M. Gettys, *How to Teach the Bible* (Richmond: John Knox Press, 1955); J.P. Love, *How to Read the Bible* (2nd. ed., NewYork: Macmillan, 1951); G. Campbell Morgan, *The Study and Teaching of the English Bible* (New York: Fleming H. Revell, 1910); Wilbur M. Smith, *Profitable Bible Study* (Boston: W.A. Wilde, 1939); Patrick Fairbairn, *Hermeneutical Manual* (Philadelphia: Smith English, 1859); and Milton S. Terry, *Biblical Hermeneutics* (New York: Eaton Mains, 1907). Perhaps the most helpful of all is Robert A. Traina's *Methodical Bible Study* (especially chapter 2), upon which the following text is partially dependent. A good short discussion of interpretive problems of the Creationists with special emphasis upon their neglect of spiritual community is Lawrence Boadt, "The Theologian," *Academe*, 68 (March/April 1982): 17-20.

(3) Conrad Hyers, "Biblical Literalism: Constricting the Cosmic Dance," *The Christian Century*, 99 (August, 1982): 823.

(4) There are many biblical passages that express the relationship of God and truth. Deuteronomy 32:4 indicates that he is a God of truth without iniquity; II Samuel 7:28 indicates that Jehovah's word is truth and that he promises goodness; Psalm 146:6, an especially relevant passage, attributes to God the making of heaven and earth (all there is) which keeps (expresses) truth forever; Hebrews 6:18 affirms that it is impossible for God to lie. There are many others.

(5) Cited in Thomas Winship, *Zetetic Cosmogony* (Durban, South Africa: T.L. Cullingworth, 1899), 144.

(6) National Academy of Sciences, *Science and Creationism* (Washington, D.C.: National Academy Press, 1984), 6.

(7) The most unfortunate situation has involved Paul Ellwanger, the leader of Citizens for Fairness in Education. He is the father of the legal drive for passage of equal time

provisions on the state level. In concert with other Creationists he has sought to differentiate scientific creationism from Biblical creationism, stating that the scientific version can stand apart from the Bible. Yet, in his private correspondence concerning the Arkasas Creation Trial, which has become a matter of public record, he freely admits that the Bible is the source of the model. There is a serious ethical question of whether the intention is deception if one really believes the Bible is the source, and yet it is presented as a non-religious concept.

(8) Henry M. Morris, *The Genesis Record* (Grand Rapids: Baker Book House, 1976), xii and 22 .

Chapter 6

(1) Larson, *Trial and Error*, 93.

(2) Larson, *Trial and Error*, 94.

(3) Norman L. Geisler, *The Creator in the Courtroom: 'Scopes II'* (Milford, MI: Mott Media, 1982), 18.

(4) Larson, *Trial and Error*, 94

(5) Larson, *Trial and Error*, 95.

(6) Larson, *Trial and Error*, 99.

(7) Larson, *Trial and Error*, 103.

(8) Larson, *Trial and Error*, 107.

(9) Larson, *Trial and Error*, 117.

(10) Larson, *Trial and Error*, 135.

(11) Larson, *Trial and Error*, 140.

(12) Peter David, "Texan Textbooks Evolve," *Nature* 308 (April 19, 1984), 680.

(13) Robert M. O'Neil, "Creationism, Curriculum, and the Constitution," *Academe* 68 (March/April 1982): 22. See also Fred Edwords, "The Current Controversy," *The Humanist* 42 (January/February l982): 46.

(14) Geisler, *The Creator in the Courtroom*, 3.

(15) Larson, *Trial and Error*, 154.

(16) Geisler, *The Creator in the Courtroom*, 207-8 and 218. For a perception from the opposite side see Janet Raloff, "Of God and Darwin," *Science News* 121 (January 2, 1982): 12-13.

(17) Raloff, "Of God and Darwin," 12-13.

(18) Larson, *Trial and Error*, 160.

(19) Larson, *Trial and Error*, 163.

(20) Larson, *Trial and Error*, 162. See also Roger Lewin, "Texas Repeals Antievolution Rules," *Science* 224 (April 27, 1984): 370. The latter account exposed the pressures applied by the People for the American Way.

(21) Fred Edwords, "The Aftermath of Arkansas," *The Humanist* 42 (March/April 1982): 55.

(22) "Creationism Defeated in Louisiana Senate," *Science* 224 (June 8, 1984): 1079. See also *Science* 225 (July 6, 1984): 36, and Roger Lewin, "Creationism Downed Again in Louisiana," *Science* 231 (January 10, 1986): 112.

(23) Larson, *Trial and Error*, 165. See also Stephen Budiansky, "Creationism Thwarted," *Nature* 300 (December 2, 1982): 394.

(24) Lewin, "Creationism Downed," 112.

(25) Cheryl M. Fields, "72 Nobel Laureates Join Plea to Supreme Court to Quash 'Creation-Science' Law," *The Chronicle of Higher Education* 33 (September 3, 1986): 74. See also "72 Nobelists Protest 'Creation Science'" *Presbyterian Journal* 4 (September 10, 1986): 4.

(26) "Text of the Opinion," *The United States Law Week* (June 6, 1987) 4860.

(27) Fred Edwords, "The Turning Tide," *The Humanist* 44 (July/August 1984): 35.

(28) Tim Beardsley, "California Setback for Evolutionists," *Nature* 317 (September 5, 1985): 3.

(29) The censorship claim is a common one; for example, lobbying by the Gablers is censorship, while lobbying by People for the American Way is fighting for freedom. See Fred Edwords, "Textbook Censorship," *The Humanist* 43 (July/August 1983): 35.

(30) Nelkin, *The Creation Controversy*, 65. See also Mel and Norma Gabler, *What Are They Teaching Our Children?* (Wheaton, IL: Victor Books, 1985).

(31) Dorothy Nelkin, *Science Textbook Controversies and the Politics of Equal Time* (Cambridge: MIT Press, 1977), 42.

(32) Nelkin, *The Creation Controversy*, 66.

(33) Frederick Edwords, "Why Bother With the Creationists?" *The Humanist*, 44 (January/February 1984): 36.

(34) Edwords, "Why Bother With the Creationists?" 44. See also Kim McDonald, "Forced Teaching of Creationism Threatens Integrity of Education," *The Chronicle of Higher Education* 23 (January 13, 1982): 10.

(35) Robert M. O'Neil, "Creationism, Curriculum and the Constitution," *Academe* 68 (March/April 1982): 21.

(36) Frederick Edwords, "Upgrading Science Education in Texas," *The Humanist* 45 (January/February 1985), 30.

(37) Frederick Edwords, "The Battle Goes Underground," *The Humanist* 44 (September/October 1984): 38.

(38) Kendrick Frazier, "Creationists Lose in Florida, *The Skeptical Inquirer* 10 (Summer 1986): 298.

(39) Kendrick Frazier, "Evolution in Science Texts: Ups and Downs in California," *The Skeptical Inquirer* 10 (Spring, 1986): 18-19. A more extended discussion of the initial action appears in Tim Beardsley, "Californian Setback for Creationists," *Nature* 317 (September 5, 1985): 3.

(40) "Biology in Texas," *The Christian Century* 106 (June 7-14, 1989) 584.

(41) The last column was Edwords, "Seeing the Light." The column had been initiated by Frederick Edwords, "The Current Controversy," *The Humanist* 42 (January/February, 1982): 46-7.

(42) Edwords, "The Battle Goes Underground," 38. See also Cheryl M. Fields, "College Backed in Creationism Dispute," *The Chronicle of Higher Education* 24 (April 21, 1982).

CHAPTER 7

(1) This perception is compatible with the conclusions of Tim Stafford, "Cease-Fire in the Laboratory," *Christianity Today* 31 (April 3, 1987): 18.

(2) Ronald Strahan, "Ex nihilo ad absurdum," *Search* 12, no. 7 (July 1981): 189.

(3) A textbook which carries this to an extreme is C. Leon Harris, *Evolution: Genesis and Revelations* (Albany: State University of New York Press, 1981). The sarcasm is so strong that this book is seldom cited by other authors opposed to Creationism, perhaps

Notes   155

indicating the extent of verbal excess. Arthur J. Boucet called Creationists scientific prostitutes and as crooked as a three dollar bill. See Henry P. Zuidema, "Teaching Scientific Creationism of Campus: Is the Controversy Cooling?" *Academic Freedom* (January/February 1985), 8.

(4) John William Draper, *History of the Conflict between Religion and Science* (New York: Appleton, 1874); Andrew Dickson White, *A History of the Warfare of Science with Theology in Christendom*, 2 vols. (New York: Appleton, 1896).

(5) The best historiographical essay on the "warfare" thesis and subsequent movements is Numbers, "Science and Religion," 59-80. The persistence of the warfare hypothesis among non-historians is illustrated by Arnold and Hulda Grobman, "Creationism: Fight with Evolution an Ancient One," *Saint Louis Post-Dispatch* (December 4, 1986), Section B, 1. Arnold Grobman is former Chancellor of the University of Missouri-St. Louis. This article recounts the "perversion" of science by the Church, including long discounted accounts of the Galileo affair.

(6) Robert K. Merton, *Science, Technology, and Society in Seventeenth Century England* (repr. New York: Harper Torchbooks, 1970).

(7) See Reijer Hooykaas, *Religion and the Rise of Modern Science* (Grand Rapids: Eerdmans, 1972); Stanley L. Jaki, *The Road of Science and the Ways of God* (Chicago: University of Chicago Press, 1978); and *Science and Creation* (New York: Science History Publishing, 1974). See also Eugene M. Klaaren, *Religious Origins of Modern Science* (Grand Rapids: Eerdmans, 1977).

(8) Nils Eldredge, for example, simply says that science is not a belief system. See *The Monkey Business* (New York: Washington Square Press, 1982), 22.

(9) Robert J. Twiss, "Science and Creationism,' *Science News* 111 (April 30, 1977): 13.

(10) Harris, *Evolution: Genesis and Revelations*, 7.

(11) Harris, *Evolution: Genesis and Revelations*, 8-11.

(12) Harris, *Evolution: Genesis and Revelations*, 15

(13) Harris, *Evolution: Genesis and Revelations*, 16.

(14) Harris, *Evolution: Genesis and Revelations*, 162.

(15) An example of this is Frederick Edwords' labeling of Davis A. Young as a Creationist, although Young has written a major work (*Christianity and the Age of the Earth*) refuting the young Earth and the idea that all of geology can be explained as a result of the Genesis flood.

(16) National Academy of Sciences, *Science and Creationism*, 15, 18.

(17) National Academy of Sciences, *Science and Creationism*, 17.

(18) National Academy of Sciences, *Science and Creationism*, 7.

(19) Mark A. Noll, "Christian World Views and Some Lessons of History," in Arthur Holmes, ed., *The Making of a Christian Mind* (Downers Grove, IL: InterVarsity Press, 1985), 49-51.

(20) The essentials of early Darwinism were as follows: (1) In any given geographic region more life forms come into existence than the environment can support. (2) No two organisms are alike, and the random variations can be transmitted. (3) In the struggle for existence, advantageous differences allow their possessors to survive. (4) Winners in the struggle to survive transmit their characteristics by heredity.

(21) Peter J. Bowler, *The Eclipse of Darwinism* (Baltimore: John Hopkins University Press, 1983), 16.

(22) Examples of those adopting such a position would be Asa Gray, G. Frederick Wright, James McCosh of Princeton and Oren Root of Missouri. See Ronald L. Numbers, "G. Frederick Wright: From Christian Darwinist to Fundamentalist" *ISIS* 79 (1988): 624-45,

and Win Winship, "Oren Root, Darwinism and Biblical Criticism," *Journal of Presbyterian History* 62 (Summer 1984): 115.

(23) For excellent brief accounts (although unsympathetic to any Christian perspective) and short excerpts from original sources concerning the arrival of Darwinism in the American intellectual climate, see George H. Daniels, ed., *Darwinism Comes to America* (Waltham, MA: Blaisdell Publishing, 1968).

(24) An especially helpful survey of the rewriting of textbooks is chapter 1, "Evolution in American Education Before 1920," in Larson, *Trial and Error*, 7-27.

(25) Larson, *Trial and Error*, 10.

(26) Larson, *Trial and Error*, 13.

(27) For a complete account of Shaler's role in promoting Darwinism and for the content of his religious beliefs, consult David N. Livingstone, *Nathaniel Southgate Shaler and the Culture of American Science* (Tuscaloosa: The University of Alabama Press, 1987).

(28) Numbers, "Science and Religion." Also helpful is the more extensive work of David N. Livingstone that is based in part upon Numbers' work: *Darwin's Forgotten Defenders: The Encounter Between Evangelical Theology and Evolutionary Thought* (Grand Rapids: Eerdmans, 1987).

(29) Bowler, *The Eclipse of Darwinism*, 204.

(30) Numbers, "Science and Religion," 627-8.

(31) B.F. Skinner, *Beyond Freedom and Dignity* (New York: Knopf, 1971).

(32) ASA, *Teaching Science*, 34.

(33) ASA, *Teaching Science*, 34.

(34) ASA, *Teaching Science*, 28.

(35) Jim Brooks, *Origins of Life* (Belleville, MI: Lion Publishing, 1985), 80-120.

CHAPTER 8

(1) These affirmations are very similar to those of the editorial, "Guideposts for the Current Debate Over Origins," *Christianity Today* 26 (October 8, 1982): 22. In 1910 James Orr declared that the Bible was not an "interpretive textbook of natural science." See *The Faith of a Modern Christian* (London: Hodder and Stoughton, 1910), 206.

(2) William J. Bennetta, "Creationism: Response and Comments," *Pacific Discovery* 38 (April-June 1985): 7.

(3) Arnold D. Ehlert, "Foreword," in Henry M. Morris, *The Genesis Record* (Grand Rapids: Baker Book House, 1976), v.

(4) A short summary of the various interpretations of the meaning of day in Genesis One is given in "Guideposts for the Current Debate Over Origins," 24.

(5) G. Frederick Wright, *Studies in Science and Religion* (Andover, MA: Draper, 1882) 352-4.

(6) This has been recognized for over 900 years—the commentator Rashi (c. 1000 A.D.) clearly stated that the first verses of Genesis were not intended to state the order of the creation. See Harry M. Orlinski, "The Plain Meaning of Genesis 1:1-3," *Biblical Archaeologist* (December 1983), 208.

(7) There is a further problem with assuming that the order is scientific here. The order in Genesis One is identical to that of the Enuma Elish, the Babylonian creation story. Extant copies of the Enuma Elish date to approximately 1000 B.C., but many scholars presume the document to antedate 2000 B.C. One possibility is that Genesis One is borrowed from the Enuma Elish and turned into a refutation of the polytheism of the Babylonian document,

which would impart scientific accuracy to it. The other alternative is that the Babylonian myth was borrowed from the Hebrew account, which would make it much older than Moses. If it were this old and an oral tradition of a nomadic people, it seems doubtful that the order would necessarily convey scientific accuracy. See Ralph H. Elliott, *The Message of Genesis* (Nashville: Broadman Press, 1961), 21-25.

(8) Hyers, "Biblical Literalism," 825. The structure and symbolic significance are readily agreed upon by theologians of all persuasions. In addition to several conservative commentaries, a more liberal affirmation may be found in Frederick A. Filby, *Creation Revealed* (New York: Revell, 1963), 17-8. Orlinski also points out that "heaven and earth" is the biblical term used for the world, or universe, all that there is. See Orlinski, 208.

(9) This has been noted by numerous biblical scholars, and even by the Christian physicist Joseph Spradley in "A Christian View of the Physical World," in Arthur Holmes, ed., *The Making of a Christian Mind,* 58. Spradley calls the order significant for "ritual," but this author believes that significance for use as a catechism is better. The Catholic scholar Richard J. Clifford, S.J. indirectly affirms this in his discussion of the doctrine of creation in "The Hebrew Scriptures and the Theology of Creation," *Theological Studies* 46 (1985): 507-23.

(10) Conrad Hyers, "Biblical Literalism: Constricting the Cosmic Dance," *The Christian Century* 99 (August 11, 1982): 826.

(11) That science opposes Christianity is the clear import of the sermon entitled "The Collapse of Evolution," by D. James Kennedy, delivered at Coral Ridge Presbyterian Church, Fort Lauderdale, Florida on September 27, 1981. Kennedy indicates that secular humanism and communism are founded on evolution. Should it fail, they would fall as well. Secular humanism and communism are the primary sources of atheism and the tide of immorality in the world, he says. It is surprising that a biological theory can do so much.

(12) Einstein himself initially rejected the implications of an expanding universe, for it seemed to point clearly to a beginning, too close to the Christian conception. Spradley, 71.

(13) Most of the so-called dark companions of stars discovered so far are much larger in proportion to their star than Jupiter is to the Sun, which has caused most astronomers to conclude that they are dim companions in binary star systems.

(14) A popular and somewhat sensational account of the seamier side of science is available in William Broad and Nicholas Wade, *Betrayers of the Truth: Fraud and Deceit in the Halls of Science* (New York: Simon and Schuster, 1982).

(15) Oren Root, a frontier Presbyterian who sought to save the bonds of religion and science, attributed the conflicts not to "real disharmony" but to limited human understanding of both Bible and science, and to "pride of reason" on the part of both scientist and theologian. Winship, "Oren Root, Darwinism and Biblical Criticism," 111 and 114.

(16) Laurie R. Godfrey, "The Flood of Anti-evolutionism," *Natural History* 90 (June 1981): 9.

(17) Charles B. Thaxton, Walter L. Bradley and Roger L. Olsen, *The Mystery of Life's Origin: Reassessing Current Theories* (New York: Philosophical Library Publishers, 1984).

(18) Reginald M. Gorczynski and E.J. Steele, "Simultaneous Yet Independent Inheritance of Somatically Acquired Tolerance to Two Distinct H-2 Anti-Genic Haplotype Determinants in Mice," *Nature* 289 (February 19, 1981): 678-81. The editorial was entitled "Too Soon for the Rehabilitation of Lamarck," 631.

(19) Stuart W. Hughes, "Brontosaurus in the Congo?" *Creation/Evolution* 12 (Spring, 1983): 36-7.

(20) Duane Gish confidently affirms that "...there is no such thing that could be legitimately called theistic evolution" in "It Is Either 'In the Beginning God'—or—'...Hydrogen,'" *Christianity Today* 26 (October 8, 1982): 28. Calling theistic evolution

theologically bankrupt betrays a poor spirit. Name-calling is a frequent resort when the well of effective argument runs dry.

(21) Conrad Hyers, "Biblical Literalism, 824.

(22) Oren Root, "Thanksgiving Sermon," Glasgow, Missouri, 1874, Oren Root Papers, 1858-1930, Western Historical Manuscripts Collection, State Historical Society of Missouri, Columbia Missouri, Folder 1, page 9.

Index of Name